Legal Thought and Eastern Orthodox Christianity

Ecumenical Patriarch Bartholomew I, the spiritual leader of Eastern Orthodox Christians worldwide, has thought profoundly about the role of law as it applies to the church, to civic life in Europe, to human rights, to religious freedom, and to the environment. In this book, leading scholars across the world reflect critically on the significance of his legal thought for human flourishing, for Christian social teaching, and for Christian unity. His legal thought is summed up in five key public addresses that he has delivered around the world in recent years, on: church law as an ecumenical instrument; the role of religion in a changing Europe; Orthodoxy and human rights; religion and freedom; and climate change, ecumenical imperatives. The collection presents critical reflections on the legal thought in these five important, distinct, and topical fields of human life. Its ten chapters, with two chapters devoted to each of his five addresses, are written by leading scholars across the world from different Christian traditions with expertise in the fields studied. They provide an analysis of the legal thought of the Patriarch, explain its significance legally, theologically, and politically, and propose its unifying value for the whole of global Christianity today. The book will be essential reading for academics and researchers working in the areas of law and religion, legal philosophy, comparative canon law, theology, and ecumenical studies.

Norman Doe is Professor and Director, Centre for Law and Religion, Cardiff Law School, Academic Bencher, Inner Temple, and Chancellor, Diocese of Bangor, Church in Wales.

Aetios Nikiforos, The Very Rev Grand Ecclesiarch, is Director of the Private Office of Ecumenical Patriarch Bartholomew, Secretary of the Synodal Commissions on Canon Law Issues and on Inter-Orthodox Affairs, and Doctoral Candidate in Canon Law at Cardiff University.

Law and Religion

The practice of religion by individuals and groups, the rise of religious diversity, and the fear of religious extremism, raise profound questions for the interaction between law and religion in society. The regulatory systems involved, the religion laws of secular government (national and international) and the religious laws of faith communities, are valuable tools for our understanding of the dynamics of mutual accommodation and the analysis and resolution of issues in such areas as: religious freedom; discrimination; the autonomy of religious organisations; doctrine, worship and religious symbols; the property and finances of religion; religion, education and public institutions; and religion, marriage and children. In this series, scholars at the forefront of law and religion contribute to the debates in this area. The books in the series are analytical with a key target audience of scholars and practitioners, including lawyers, religious leaders, and others with an interest in this rapidly developing discipline.

Titles in this series include:

Christianity, Ethics and the Law
The Concept of Love in Christian Legal Thought
Edited by Zachary R. Calo, Joshua Neoh and A. Keith Thompson

Law and Christianity in Poland
The Legacy of the Great Jurists
Edited by Franciszek Longchamps de Bérier and Rafael Domingo

Democracy, Religion, and Commerce
Private Markets and the Public Regulation of Religion
Edited by Kathleen Flake and Nathan B. Oman

For more information about this series, please visit: www.routledge.com/Law-and-Religion/book-series/LAWRELIG

Legal Thought and Eastern Orthodox Christianity

The Addresses of Ecumenical Patriarch Bartholomew I

Edited by Norman Doe and Aetios Nikiforos

Routledge
Taylor & Francis Group
LONDON AND NEW YORK

First published 2024
by Routledge
4 Park Square, Milton Park, Abingdon, Oxon OX14 4RN

and by Routledge
605 Third Avenue, New York, NY 10158

Routledge is an imprint of the Taylor & Francis Group, an informa business

British Library Cataloguing-in-Publication Data
A catalogue record for this book is available from the British Library

ISBN: 978-1-032-61037-5 (hbk)
ISBN: 978-1-032-63673-3 (pbk)
ISBN: 978-1-032-63674-0 (ebk)

DOI: 10.4324/9781032636740

Typeset in Galliard
by Deanta Global Publishing Services, Chennai, India

Contents

Foreword

In the work and teaching of Ecumenical Patriarch Bartholomew, a global personality is reflected, and the faith and knowledge of the Orthodox Church are combined with moral and practical reason. The background of his public interventions is his solid and multifaceted legal education, which has canon law as its epistemological basis and research focus. At the same time, his thinking extends and deepens into the most topical and critical issues of institutions and rights, such as the place of religious freedom in a multicultural and pluralistic Europe, the connection between the values of Orthodoxy and environmental awareness, as well as the response to the climate crisis, and the contemporary delimitation of the relationship between Church and State in a mutually beneficial way. In His All Holiness' ecumenical discourse, the great secular quandaries are illuminated by the Christian Orthodox tradition and its timeless principles: love, equality, and justice, so that Oneself contains the Other. Human dignity, the foundation of our legal system, with its theological roots, constitutes our unsurpassed horizon in the search for our common path and place. In the words of the Patriarch,

> Many today place their hopes in science; others in politics; others in technology. But none of these can guarantee the future if man has not embraced the preaching of reconciliation, love, and justice, the preaching of acceptance of the other, of the different, even of the enemy.

The present volume, by highlighting the legal dimension of his rich thought, is an excellent contribution to the enlightenment of this great personality of our time.

Katerina Sakellaropoulou,
President of the Hellenic Republic

Preface

The stimulus for this book was the 50th anniversary, which occurs in December 2023, of Ecumenical Patriarch Bartholomew's episcopal election and ordination. However, in no way should this book be treated as a *festschrift*, because it is not. A more accurate description of this project would be to identify it as the product of 'laboratory' work.

We start with the fact that His All-Holiness is a jurist by training. With that in mind, our aim is to uncover his legal thought. Our focus is not Bartholomew's academic papers, because, despite their significance, they are oriented toward a limited scholarly audience. Rather, we have chosen an understudied genre, but nonetheless representative of the impact of Bartholomew's legal thinking: His Patriarchal addresses.

This book brings together for the first time in a single volume central selected extracts from five prominent public Patriarchal addresses, in which he raises key topics on law and religion before a diverse and non-specialised audience. Each address is followed by a pair of reflections from scholars with different methodological backgrounds and Christian affiliations. The outcome is a rich collection of diverse views on Bartholomew's legal ideas, inviting the reader to think critically on broader questions about (Orthodox) Christianity and law. This book seeks to further open, and not to close such questions. We are very grateful to the contributors of this book and to Alison Kirk and her colleagues at Routledge for their support and hard work on this project.

Norman Doe
Aetios Nikiforos

Contributors

Miguel Blanco is Professor of Law and Religion at the University of Alcalá, and is a member of the European Consortium for Church and State Research.

Frank Cranmer is Honorary Research Fellow at the Centre for Law and Religion, Cardiff University, and a Fellow of St Chad's College, Durham.

Norman Doe is Professor and Director, Centre for Law and Religion, Cardiff Law School, Academic Bencher, Inner Temple, and Chancellor, Diocese of Bangor, Church in Wales.

M. Christian Green is Senior Fellow at the Center for the Study of Law and Religion at Emory University.

Christopher Hill, was Bishop successively of Stafford and Guildford in the Church of England, now retired. From the early 1970s, he was involved in official ecumenical dialogue with the Roman Catholic, Orthodox, Lutheran and Reformed Churches and was President of the Conference of European Churches. He has a special concern for the relationship between ecumenism, ecclesiology and canon law and is President of the Ecclesiastical Law Society.

Mark Hill KC is Diocesan Chancellor of Chichester, Leeds and Europe, an Honorary Professor at Cardiff University, and Visiting Professor at the University of Notre Dame.

Isidoros Katsos, a Greek Orthodox Archimandrite, is Assistant Professor of Theological Epistemology and Philosophy, Theological School, Faculty of Theology, Athens University.

Aetios Nikiforos, The Very Rev Grand Ecclesiarch, is Director of the Private Office of Ecumenical Patriarch Bartholomew, Secretary of the Synodal Commissions on Canon Law Issues and on Inter-Orthodox Affairs, and Doctoral Candidate in Canon Law at Cardiff University.

Andrea Pin is Full Professor of Comparative Law at the University of Padua in Italy.

Frederick V. Simmons is John Templeton Foundation Research Scholar at Princeton Theological Seminary.

John Witte, Jr is Woodruff University Professor and Faculty Director of the Law and Religion Center at Emory University.

Introduction

Norman Doe and Aetios Nikiforos

Bartholomew I, Archbishop of Constantinople–New Rome and Ecumenical Patriarch, is the spiritual leader of over 220 million Eastern Orthodox Christians worldwide. His All-Holiness Bartholomew is also a canon lawyer. Not only did he study for a doctorate in canon law (completed in 1970), but, throughout his ministry, he has thought profoundly about law – its nature, purposes, and impact – both in the church and wider society, including internationally. This book is designed to describe, explain, and evaluate the contribution of His All-Holiness, as a case study, as it were, to the wider field of legal thought in the Eastern Orthodox Church.

Key aspects of His All-Holiness' legal thought are summed up in five major public addresses he has delivered worldwide over recent years, on: church law; religion in a changing Europe; Orthodoxy and human rights; freedom of religion; and the environment and climate change.

To date, Bartholomew's understanding of law has not been systematically studied, in all its rich and diverse manifestations. This book presents, for the first time, critical reflections on his legal thought in these five important, distinct, and topical fields. Its ten chapters, with two complementary chapters devoted to each of his five addresses – and extracts of these are included in this book. The chapters are written by leading scholars across the world from different Christian traditions with expertise in the fields studied. They offer a critical analysis of the legal thought of the Ecumenical Patriarch in these five fields, explain its significance legally, theologically, and politically, and propose its value for Christianity and beyond.

Chapters 1 and 2 reflect on His All-Holiness' address, 'The Society for the Law of the Eastern Churches' 2019. In Chapter 1, Aetios Nikiforos explores His All-Holiness' treatment of the changeability of the ancient holy canons, from the first millennium of undivided Christendom, which still apply in the Eastern Orthodox Church. He does so in light of the Ecumenical Patriarch's doctoral thesis (on codifying these canons), and subsequent canonical thinking, especially his contribution to the Holy and Great Council of the Orthodox Church held in Crete in 2016. In

DOI: 10.4324/9781032636740-1

Chapter 2, Norman Doe contextualises what the address has to say about the *Statement of Principles of Christian Law* (Rome, 2016) issued by an Ecumenical Panel and launched at a workshop of the 11th Assembly of the World Council of Churches in 2022. Doe evaluates His All-Holiness' view that the *Statement* fills a 'canonical deficit' in ecumenism.

The second address is 'The Role of Religion in a Changing Europe' 2005. Frank Cranmer, in Chapter 3, examines how the address portrays Europe as increasingly multicultural and secularised and sees dialogue as essential to avoid interreligious strife. The chapter reflects on the treatment of religion in European Union treaties and charters, the institutional relationship between the Union and 'religion', and the principles in European Union law on religion. It then assesses His All-Holiness's contribution to the debate about religion in the future of Europe and the search for 'a happy concord' between religion and the Union. To complement this, Miguel Blanco in Chapter 4 deals critically with His All-Holiness' understanding of the various models used by States of the Union in their laws on relations between those States and religion at the national level. Blanco questions the utility of separationism (confining religion to the private sphere) and State–Church systems. He proposes cooperation between State and religion as the most appropriate approach to achieve social cohesion and peaceful coexistence as key values advocated by the Ecumenical Patriarch for national religion–State relations in Europe.

The third address is 'Orthodoxy and Human Rights' 2017. In Chapter 5, John Witte Jr explores the Patriarch's view that Orthodox Christians have historically been wary of human rights. Witte then discusses how His All-Holiness encourages Orthodox Christians to see human rights as God's gifts, and how such rights depend on Christian and other values for their basis and reform, including Orthodox theologies of conversion and *theosis*, *symphonia* and society, Church and State. Andrea Pin in Chapter 6 develops these themes. He analyses the Patriarch's views on seeking common ground, and the historic trajectory of the idea of dignity. Pin suggests that Bartholomew downplays the role and success of religious culture in human rights and, like the Patriarch, argues that the future of religion and human rights requires supporters of both to look afresh at themselves and admit they owe each other more than they may superficially believe.

The fourth address is 'Religious Freedom' 2014. In Chapter 7, Isidoros Katsos reflects on the Patriarch's understanding of religious freedom in Orthodox thought in the context of a range of issues and theological ideas. These include how the freedom may prove problematic for the Orthodox Church's self-understanding as a 'power institution', and how religious freedom may generate ambiguity for being an Orthodox in a pluralistic world. By way of contrast, in Chapter 8 Mark Hill reflects on

His All-Holiness' views on the need for ecumenical collaboration in the understanding and promotion of religious freedom. Hill deals with how the laws of traditions beyond Orthodox Christianity (Roman Catholic, Anglican, and Methodist) and the World Council of Churches deal with religious freedom under national and international law.

The fifth address is 'Climate Change: An Ecumenical Imperative' 2021. Christian Green in Chapter 9 assesses the thought of 'The Green Patriarch' on the environment and climate change through the lens of international law and policy. She studies how his thinking relates to the social ethics of Orthodox Christianity and ideas of self-restraint, self-emptying, equity, and justice. Green then explores how these may inform doctrines and principles of environmental law. In contrast, Frederick Simmons in Chapter 10 offers a theological reflection on His All-Holiness' thinking on the environment and climate change. He unpacks how Bartholomew recalibrates Orthodox concepts of God's creation and human moral duties in light of COVID-19, qualifies this around anthropogenic climate change, and studies ecumenical aspects of working with and learning from others – all in the context of the document *For the Life of the World* (2020).

At the end of the book, Bishop Christopher Hill reflects on the chapters and the themes in them.

It is hoped that the book will enable readers to reflect critically on the Ecumenical Patriarch's legal thought in these fields by providing an objective description of his ideas, an explanation of them, and an evaluation of his ideas from theological, political, and juridical perspectives.

Address I

Canon Law and Christian Law

The Society for the Law of the Eastern Churches 50 Years Later and the Ecumenical Movement
(Pontifical Oriental Institute, Rome, 16 September 2019)

... Here the juridical instruments of the Churches – their canons, laws, or other regulatory documents and provisions – are not treated merely as 'borders' that define the 'limits of the Church' ... For the Society, the canons are not juridical walls between the separated Churches that distinguish those within the Church from those outside of it.

On the contrary, for us the ecclesial regulatory instruments are considered as essential components for the advancement of the ecumenical movement and as inseparable from the quest for agreement at the level of doctrine, achieved through theological debate, which has been so far the principal and dominant focus in contemporary ecumenical discourse. To put it in the words of the renowned 20th-century canonist Fr. Nicolas Afanasiev,

> canons are a kind of canonical interpretation of the dogmas for a particular moment of the Church's historical existence ... Dogmas are absolute truths and canons are applications of these truths for the historical existence of the Church ... The truth that canons express is in itself absolute, yet the content of canons is not this truth itself, but the mode through which this truth must be expressed in a given historical form of the Church's life. Canons express the eternal in the temporal.[1]

1 Nicolas Afanasiev, 'The Church's Canons: Changeable or Unchangeable?', in *Tradition Alive: On the Church and the Christian Life in Our Time/ Readings from the Eastern Church*, Michael Plekon ed. (Lanham, MA: Rowman & Littlefield Publishers, Inc., 2003), 31–45, at 37–38.

DOI: 10.4324/9781032636740-2

In our doctoral dissertation we argued, and in our address at the Society's inaugural Congress we had the opportunity to reiterate, that the ancient canons

> contain the guiding and fundamental principles, on which all legislative work of the Church, created by changing ecclesiastical circumstances, must be based. The Church's legislation must always aim: firstly, at the application of the above-mentioned principles in accordance with the special needs of the Church in a given age, and secondly, at the elaboration of these principles in specific appropriate canons.[2]

These canonical principles have a theological content and are fundamental to the Church's ecclesiological self-understanding. They have a living force and contain within themselves the possibility of further development and articulation. They form a dynamic canonical tradition, 'which is the living experience of the whole body of the Church, and not a museum piece, expressing the demands of each time'.[3]

Through the comparative study of the various juridical instruments of the Churches which Article 4 of the Society's Bylaws invites us to undertake, it is possible to explore critically the extent to which different Christian traditions share common principles in their canons and other instruments of internal governance, to formulate such common principles of Christian law, and to examine the ways in which these common principles may contribute creatively to the ecumenical endeavour to enhance fuller visible unity.

This past March we had the chance to be personally informed at the Ecumenical Patriarchate about the significant canonical work of an ecumenical panel of religious leaders, jurists and theologians from ten Christian traditions worldwide … The outcome of the research work of this panel has been a *Statement of Principles of Christian Law* (2016) … These *Principles* were induced from similarities drawn precisely from a comparative study of the regulatory instruments of the participating Christian canonical traditions.

We express our gladness that a special workshop within the framework of this Congress is dedicated to this important *Statement*, which is a means of unity and collaboration between Christians of different traditions …

2 Bartholomew Archondonis, 'A Common Code for the Orthodox Churches', *Kanon* 1 (1973) 45–53, at 46.

3 See this statement of the then Metropolitan of Philadelphia (current Ecumenical Patriarch) Bartholomew at the Second Pre-Conciliar Pan-Orthodox Conference (Chambésy, 1982) in *Συνοδικά VII: Β' Προσυνοδική Πανορθόδοξος Διάσκεψις (Σαμπεζύ, 3–12 Σεπτεμβρίου 1982)* (Chambésy: Orthodox Center of the Ecumenical Patriarchate, 1994), 104.

We congratulate the Organizing Committee of this Congress for the inclusion within its proceedings of a discussion about this project, which is designed to fill the historical juridical deficit in the ecumenical enterprise. This discussion is not only very pertinent to the Congress's theme about 'how canon law assists in the ecumenical dialogue', but it also shows the Society's commitment to the promotion of its purposes through the engagement with up-to-date topics, such as 'juridical ecumenism', i.e. the study and practical deployment of canons and other regulatory instruments of churches on ecumenism.[4]

The Orthodox Church, being faithful to its ecumenical nature, deems juridical ecumenism as crucial for the promotion of the various theological dialogues ..., in which we have been engaged during the past decades. In June 2016, the Holy and Great Council of the Orthodox Church, which took place in Crete with the participation of 10 out of the then 14 local Autocephalous Churches, adopted six documents. One of these documents, entitled 'The Relations of the Orthodox Church with the Rest of the Christian World', underscored the necessity of the inter-Christian dialogues in general and the duty of the Orthodox Church to participate in them, as an expression of Orthodoxy's 'self-consciousness' ... As it is prescribed in the above-mentioned Cretan document, the basis for conducting these theological dialogues are 'the canonical principles of Orthodox ecclesiology and the canonical criteria of the already established Church Tradition', 'inspired by common fundamental principles of the Gospel'. Thus, the Orthodox Church recognises not only the centrality of the principles of canon law for its participation in the ecumenical dialogue, but also the existence of fundamental principles shared by all Christians.

Reference to 'the principles of the holy canons' is also made in another document of the Holy and Great Council, the one about 'The Sacrament of Marriage and its Impediments'. In this case, too, the principles are employed in relation to a topic that affects the ecumenical relations: mixed marriages of Orthodox Christians with non-Orthodox Christians. The principles derived from the canons are used as guides by the Holy Synod of each local Autocephalous Church during its decision-making process with regard to the 'exercise of ecclesiastical οἰκονομία in relation to impediments to marriage'.

...

The Holy Great Church of Christ, upholding the 'pan-Orthodox consensus', is the protector and guarantor of the canonical tradition of the Orthodox Church, faithfully preserving its first principles in order to

4 For juridical ecumenism see Norman Doe, 'Juridical Ecumenism', *Ecclesiastical Law Journal* 14 (2012) 195–234.

offer them anew to the ecumenical dialogue, contributing crucially to a dynamic renewal of the canonical consciousness of the Church, which is so vital for both the intra-Orthodox and inter-Christian relations, always with respect to the canonical traditions of the other Churches in their legitimate diversities.

1 The Canonist Patriarch

His All-Holiness Bartholomew and the Development of Canon Law

Aetios Nikiforos

The celebration of the 50th anniversary of His All-Holiness Ecumenical Patriarch Bartholomew's election and ordination to the holy episcopacy, on 18 and 25 December 2023, respectively, offers a unique opportunity for reflection on his long-term engagement with Canon Law. One might wonder, what is this special relationship of Patriarch Bartholomew with Church Law. More than the requirement prescribed in II Nicaea canon 2 for 'everyone who is to be advanced to the grade of bishop', has to be 'willing to acquire knowledge – a knowledge that should be searching and not superficial – of the sacred canons?' More than the role played by His predecessors to the Ecumenical Throne as guardians and defenders of the canonical tradition of the Orthodox Church?

The association of Bartholomew with canonical jurisprudence started long before his election as Ecumenical Patriarch in 1991, even long before his election and ordination to the holy episcopate in 1973.[1] It was during the last academic year (1960–1961) of his undergraduate studies in Theology at the Patriarchal Seminary on Halki, one of the Princes' Islands, that he decided to write his BA thesis on the topic of the reconstitution of a dissolved marriage.[2] Two years later, in the fall of 1963, as soon as he finished his two-year mandatory military service, deacon Bartholomew started his doctoral studies in Canon Law at the Pontifical Oriental Institute of the Pontifical Gregorian University in Rome.[3] 1963 is, thus, the year that symbolically marks the beginning of Bartholomew's formal-academic relationship with the canonical discipline.

1 For the Patriarchal biography see Archbishop Makarios of Australia, 'His All-Holiness Ecumenical Patriarch Bartholomew, Archbishop of Constantinople and New Rome. Brief Biography' in *Βαρθολομαίῳ τῷ Οἰκουμενικῷ Πατριάρχῃ εὐλαβικόν ἀφιέρωμα* [*Reverential Dedication to the Ecumenical Patriarch Bartholomew*] (Sydney: Holy Archdiocese of Australia Publication, 2021) 101–145.

2 See Dimitrios Archondonis, *Ἀνασύστασις λυθέντος γάμου* [*The Reconstitution of a Dissolved Marriage*] (Halki, 1961; unpublished thesis).

3 For the Pontifical Oriental Institute see V. Poggi, S.J., *Per la Storia del Pontificio Istituto Orientale* [*On the History of the Pontifical Oriental Institute*] (Rome: Pontificio Istituto Orientale, 2000).

DOI: 10.4324/9781032636740-3

Therefore, alongside the 50th anniversary of His All-Holiness' election and ordination to the episcopate, it is also very fitting to celebrate this year the 60th anniversary of his engagement with Canon Law. We must honour along with the 'green Patriarch'[4] and 'the Patriarch of solidarity',[5] the 'canonist Patriarch', an unknown title of Ecumenical Patriarch Bartholomew, which reflects a neglected, but equally important aspect of his 50-year long sacrificial episcopal ministry to the Holy Great Church of Christ.

And what better way to pay tribute to such a significant anniversary than a reflection upon the Keynote Address that His All-Holiness gave on 16 September 2019, on the occasion of another 50th anniversary: of the founding of the Society for the Law of the Eastern Churches, celebrated in Rome with the Society's 24th International Congress. During the Congress' inaugural session, at the Pontifical Oriental Institute, Bartholomew, founding Vice-President of the Society, had the unique opportunity to return to his *alma mater* to offer a reflection not only on the past 50 years of the Society's life, work and accomplishments, but also on his vision about the Society's future, focussing on the role of Canon Law in the advancement of the ecumenical dialogue.

I. The Role of Principles in Canon Law

In his address, the Ecumenical Patriarch emphasised that the regulatory instruments of the various Christian traditions should not be treated as juridical walls that keep separate the one Church from the other. On the contrary, inspired by the Society's By-Laws, he encouraged the comparative study of these Church regulations with the purpose of examining their degree of convergence, as reflected in the fundamental principles that they share. At this point, Bartholomew explained that in the Eastern Orthodox canonical tradition these fundamental principles are contained in the ancient canons, which comprise the Byzantine corpus. He described these principles as having 'a theological content' and as being 'fundamental to the Church's ecclesiological self-understanding'. And he continued by underlining that 'they have a living force and contain within themselves the possibility of further development and articulation'. As two examples of the principles' further development, the Patriarch mentioned (a) their application by the ecclesiastical legislation 'in accordance with the special needs of the Church in a given time' and (b) their elaboration into 'specific appropriate canons'.

4 This title was formalised in 1997 in the White House by the then Vice-President of the United States, Al Gore.

5 See J. Chryssavgis and K. Delikostantis, *The Patriarch of Solidarity* (Istanbul, 2016).

The Patriarch copied these last two quotations from his address at the inaugural Congress of the Society for the Law of the Eastern Churches, back in 1971. The then-young Doctor of Canon Law Archimandrite Bartholomew Archondonis presented a paper on the need for 'A Common Code for the Orthodox Churches'.[6] This paper was a summarised version of all the main points from his doctoral dissertation, entitled *On the Codification of the Sacred Canons and the Canonical Institutions in the Orthodox Church*,[7] which was successfully defended at the Pontifical Oriental Institute in 1968, under the mentorship and supervision of the Slovenian Jesuit Eastern Catholic priest and Professor of Canon Law, Ivan Žužek, a renown canonist and specialist in the field of the codification, who was then also serving as Rector of the Institute (1967–1973).[8] The choice of His All-Holiness to make an explicit reference to his dissertation and paper was not a mere symbolic gesture to pay tribute to the Society's Inaugural Congress, but it primarily signalled his treatment of his doctoral monograph as a constant point of reference and reflection upon the essence of his canonical thought.

Therefore, in order to analyse and evaluate this position of His All-Holiness with regard to the notion of development in Canon Law, his doctorate is an essential primary source and aid of great value, the document par excellence that still contains his fundamental presuppositions and standards as a canonist.[9] These canonical standards have remained the same throughout all these years and the Ecumenical Patriarch holds them dear to his heart and weighs them carefully every time he takes a decision. This is something admitted not only by his admirers, but also by his critics, who go back to his 1970 dissertation in order to claim the consistency and continuity between what the Archimandrite Bartholomew wrote there and his actions as Ecumenical Patriarch.

6 See Bartholomew Archondonis, 'A Common Code for the Orthodox Churches', 1 *Kanon* (1973) 45–53.

7 Bartholomew Archondonis, *Περὶ τὴν κωδικοποίησιν τῶν ἱ. κανόνων καὶ τῶν κανονικῶν διατάξεων ἐν τῇ Ὀρθοδόξῳ Ἐκκλησίᾳ* [*On the Codification of the Sacred Canons and the Canonical Institutions in the Orthodox Church*] (Thessaloniki: Patriarchal Institute for Patristic Studies, 1970).

8 See C. Vasil S.J., 'Ivan Žužek S.J. (1924–2004) e il contributo scientifico alla canonistica orientale' ['Ivan Žužek S.J. (1924–2004) and the scientific contribution to eastern canon law'], 8 *Iura Orientalia* (2012) 102–141.

9 Due to space limitations, in this chapter citations are not from His All-Holiness' dissertation, which was written in Greek and excerpts from which would require translation, but only from his 1971 paper, which was originally written in English.

II. Conceptual Approaches to the Holy Canons

A prerequisite to examine and understand His All-Holiness' canonical thought would be the schematic classification of the modern Orthodox canonists into two broad categories.[10] The first consists of scholars who follow the 'legal-scientific' approach to the canons. Its proponents, who have usually received, beyond their theological formation, academic legal training as well, treat the text of the ancient canonical sources as a logical system of formal norms similar to the categories and classifications of modern civil law. For this reason, they prefer calling their discipline 'Canon Law', when they focus solely on the Church's own law, or 'Ecclesiastical Law', when they deal primarily with civil legislation on ecclesiastical matters and its relationship with Church legislation. In both cases, they consider their subject as another field of legal science, organising their manuals in a very similar way to the structure of the classical legal textbooks of the continental tradition. This approach often tends to ignore the historical, philosophical and theological dimensions of Canon Law and argues in favour of the disciplinary autonomy of law versus theology, on the ground that the latter detracts from the efficiency of the law. In this way, the 'legal-scientific' approach ends in pure legalism that places the law above the human person and the community.

The second approach, which could be called the 'historical-philosophical', denies the employment of legal categories for the study of the canons, replacing the name 'Canon Law' with the name 'Canonical Tradition' and employing the canons not as legal regulations, but as expressions of deeper metaphysical realities that have to be transcended. Its proponents are mainly theologians, historians, or philosophers, with no or limited legal training, who view the law as a hindrance to the spiritual character of the Church. In this way, the 'historical-philosophical' approach can easily yield to antinomianism, which considers law as an obstacle to individual freedom in the personal response to God, denying, thus, the role of reason in establishing the ecclesial order.

Bartholomew became influenced by both approaches, the first being more prevalent among Greek-speaking canonists, such as Hamilcar S. Alivisatos, Professor of Canon Law at the University of Athens,[11] while the second being witnessed primarily in the 19th–20th-century Russian canonical thought, with the Russian Émigré canonist Fr. Nicholas

10 These categories are inspired by D. Wagschal, *Law and Legality in the Greek East – The Byzantine Canonical Tradition* (Oxford: Oxford University Press, 2015) 12–14.

11 For Hamilcar Alivizatos see K. Mouratidis, *Ὁ Καθηγητὴς Ἀμίλκας Σπυρ. Ἀλιβιζάτος – Βίος, Δρᾶσις καὶ Συγγραφικὸν Ἔργον* [*Professor Hamilcar Spyr. Alivizatos – Life, Work and Scholarship*] (Athens, 1968; offprint).

Afanasiev, Professor of Canon Law at St Sergius Institute in Paris,[12] as its most prominent exponent. One of the works that Bartholomew cited several times in his dissertation, when dealing with the fundamental issue of whether the canons are amenable to change or not – a key question in his discussion of the revision of the canonical corpus with modification or abolition of canons – was an article by Afanasiev,[13] in which he argues that the canons as truths of divine revelation are immutable in a relative sense: they are immutable for their own age. The truth that the canons express, as the dogmatic essence of the Church, is itself absolute, and, therefore, immutable, yet their content is not this truth itself, but the mode through which this truth is expressed in a given historical form of the Church's life.[14] This main argument of Afanasiev is recited by His All-Holiness in his 2019 Keynote Address. Afanasiev sees harmony between a canon's abiding essence and its historical existence. The latter is the form in which the dogmatic essence of the Church is embodied in history. Therefore, just as in physics a force can act only if it has a point of application, in a similar manner, canons are active only to the extent they are applicable to the conditions of the Church's life for which they were enacted. If this point of application ceases to exist, then the canons, too, become inoperative and need replacement.[15]

In his dissertation, Bartholomew elaborated on Afanasiev's ideas, arguing that 'the canons would be, as dogmas are, forever unchangeable, were they based only on divine law. But the Church's law is a divino-human law, for the Church is not only invisible but visible as well'.[16] Influenced by the Roman Catholic canonical thought, the young Doctor of Canon Law expressed the opinion that:

> the only laws which are unchangeable are the fundamental laws of the Church which were formulated basically by the Lord and the Apostles, or those which are in accordance with the essence of the Church and are expressions of it. Other canons, brought into being by temporal necessities, express the essence of the Church in her various historical forms of existence. Such canons can be changed or

12 For Nicholas Afanasiev see M. Plekon, 'Nicolas Afanasiev: Explorer of the Eucharist, the Church and Life in Them' in M. Plekon, ed., *Living Icons: Persons of Faith in the Eastern Church* (Notre Dame, IN: University of Notre Dame Press, 2002) 149–177.

13 N.N. Afanasiev, 'The Canons of the Church: Changeable or Unchangeable?', 11 *St Vladimir's Seminary Quarterly* (1967) 54–68.

14 Ibid., 61–62.

15 Ibid., 62.

16 Archondonis, 'A Common Code', 46.

> even abrogated, if they do not any more serve the purpose for which they were originally issued.[17]

Nevertheless, Afanasiev rejected the distinction between divine, unchangeable, elements in Canon Law and human, changeable ones. For him, '*jus humanum* does not exist in the Church; all decisions are divinely inspired ("they are all enlightened by one and the same Spirit")'.[18] Affected by his reading of the Lutheran historian of Canon Law, Rudolf Sohm, who regarded the emergence of Canon Law as a disastrous subversion of the life of the Church, Afanasiev argued that:

> *jus humanum* infiltrates the Church as an interpretation of this historical existence. The wider the realm of *jus humanum* in the Church, the coarser the historical forms of the Church's existence become, and the more difficult it becomes for the essence of the Church to pierce through the historical fabric. The law of man, by penetrating into the Church tends to transform the Church from a divine-human organism full of grace into a legal institution. A well-known stage of development, ecclesiastical institutionalism, threatens the Church life with obvious distortions, since it threatens to suppress the Church's life in grace.[19]

Here Afanasiev echoes the typical antinomian critique of the legalistic approach to the canons, concluding with the bold statement that

> no matter how we may define law, canons in no way belong to the field of law. Everything in scripture refers to the areas of faith and morality, and Christ left no canonical definitions which would determine the structure of the Church in her historical existence.[20]

Bartholomew did not accept these opinions of Afanasiev and rejected the position of treating the Church as a solely charismatic institution 'full of grace' at the expense of reason. He repeatedly states in his dissertation that 'the Church is a divino-human organization within which the regular evolution of ecclesiastical life must be safeguarded by a Code'.[21] And he explicitly welcomes the presence of law in the Church: 'As the Church is also a visible institution with her own organization, it is natural that her

17 Ibid.
18 Afanasiev, 'The Canons', 56.
19 Ibid., 67.
20 Ibid., 60.
21 Archondonis, 'A Common Code', 49.

legislation, *sensu stricto*, should constitute the main source of her law', and, therefore, the ancient canons as the 'main and most fundamental source of Church law'.[22] Nevertheless, the Ecumenical Patriarch does not at any point fall into the realm of legalism. He never forgets that the Church, 'guided by the Holy Spirit, follows practices always tending to foster the achievement of her highest purpose, that is to say the salvation of the human souls'.[23] With this in mind, he emphasises that any changes in the canons 'should be made only when there is "*utilitas evidens*" and "*necessitas urgens*" and with the aim of serving the salvation and the progress of the peoples, as stated in the 12th canon of the Council in Trullo'.[24]

For this reason, again unlike Afanasiev, who neglected the principle of *oikonomia*,[25] Bartholomew considers *oikonomia* as 'the essence of the Orthodox Church',[26] 'a characteristic feature, a real privilege, and a precious treasure for the Church',[27] a 'basic institution … as old as the Church',[28] which 'serves this very purpose of the Church', the salvation of the people.[29] Bartholomew's understanding of *oikonomia* is an excellent example of the way that he tried to rise above the impasses of both legalism and antinomianism,[30] as dangerous extremes that diminish the ability of Canon Law to fulfil its mission. His All-Holiness harmoniously integrates faith and reason and articulates an equilibric position, which realises that while Canon Law has no power on its own to achieve salvation, it still remains necessary to the order of the Church, as a means for faith to flourish in the lives of persons and communities in the Church.

For Bartholomew 'oikonomia is something that is lived rather than described and defined'.[31] And he continues: 'Oikonomia is an expression of love (and that is why it is not possible to define it exactly), which more than anything else is the theological virtue and organic principle of the Church'.[32] At the same time, though, avoiding antinomianism, he accepts

22 Ibid., 46.
23 Ibid., 46–47.
24 Ibid., 47.
25 See A. Nichols O.P., *The ecclesiology of N. N. Afanasiev: Patristic ressourcement and ecumenical prospect in the Russian tradition* (doctoral dissertation: University of Edinburgh, 1986) 222.
26 Bartholomeos Archondonis, 'The Problem of Oikonomia Today', 6 *Kanon* (1983) 39–50, at 49.
27 Ibid., 39.
28 Ibid.
29 Ibid., 41.
30 For legalism and antinomianism see J.J. Coughlin, *Canon Law – A Comparative Study with Anglo-American Legal Theory* (New York, NY: Oxford University Press, 2011) 3–7.
31 Archondonis, 'The Problem of Oikonomia', 40.
32 Ibid., 42.

that *oikonomia* belongs to those principles which are 'legal and canonical expressions of dogmatic truths'.[33] However, unlike the Latin concept of *dispensatio*, which, as Bartholomew clarifies is 'a legal institution applied in the same form in all the analogous cases', 'the application of oikonomia to individuals as persons, each of which has his uniqueness and particular value before God', requires the Church not to 'judge in advance and generally, but in every case separately', 'since for each of us the Son of God took flesh and was sacrificed'.[34] By applying *oikonomia* as prudent pastoral stewardship, Bartholomew maintains a balanced approach to legalism and antinomianism that restores the salvific nature of the canonical tradition, 'bringing back the lost sheep' (c.f. Trullo canon 102).

In this way, His All-Holiness highlights the important role of the canonist, as the one 'entrusted with pastoral authority' (c.f. Trullo canon 102), to go beyond the misconceptions of legalism and antinomianism, by searching out every time those fundamental norms of structure and conduct that are faithful to the mission of Canon Law, as arising from and conforming to the very nature of the Church, and by applying them to the particular needs of each time. For the Ecumenical Patriarch those norms can be found in the ancient canons, which 'contain the guiding and fundamental principles, on which all legislative work of the Church, created by changing ecclesiastical circumstances, must be based'.[35] And he continues: 'The scope for ecclesiastical legislation lies in the elaboration of these principles in the form of new canons'.[36] And: 'The new canons will formulate the new forms of the Church's existence, by which the dogmatic teachings will be expressed in the most complete manner appropriate to our age'.[37] This is Bartholomew's fundamental hermeneutic approach to Canon Law, which treats the Eastern Orthodox canonical tradition as 'dynamic', as 'the living experience of the whole body of the Church', not 'static, a museum piece', but as adapting itself to and expressing 'the demands of each time'.[38]

III. The Codification of the Sacred Canons

This same spirit characterises Bartholomew's proposal for the codification of the sacred canons. Following Alivizatos, His All-Holiness emphasises that 'we cannot talk about a real renewal of the life of the Church without

33 Ibid.
34 Ibid., 50.
35 Archondonis, 'A Common Code', 46.
36 Ibid., 51.
37 Ibid.
38 See the 2019 Keynote Address.

the revision of the Church's legislation, by means of a codification'.[39] For Bartholomew, 'the codification is mainly required for practical reasons',[40] since

> a common Code for all the Orthodox Churches would … contribute to the reinforcement of this unity that binds together the sister Orthodox Churches and foster their being seen to be one Church well organized … ready to fulfill her mission in the world with a united and consequently more widely valid legislation.[41]

For this reason, the Ecumenical Patriarch reaches even the point of arguing that 'in the creation of this disorder the Church herself has had her part to play since, in the Corpus of her canons, she has preserved canons no longer in use or applicable'.[42] And he concludes: 'in order that the Church may be realistic and vitally present in the modern world, certain canons need modifying on a more realistic and human basis'.[43]

Canons needing modification are, according to His All-Holiness, those 'canons which regulate the relations of the Orthodox to other Christians and to other religions',[44] 'pertaining to conditions and heresies which disappeared long ago'.[45] 'These canons could not have referred to later heresies or schisms or to later divisions of the Church'.[46] And he underlines: 'Today there is an ecclesiastical reality around us, which we cannot ignore. The Holy Spirit who "blows wherever he wills" (John 3,8), and is not restricted only within the history of the past, is certainly present also among heterodox'.[47]

For Bartholomew, Canon Law is significant not only for the advancement of inter-Orthodox unity, but also for the promotion of the ecumenical dialogue, which it 'can facilitate … and must not obstruct'.[48] Recognising 'the importance of Canon Law in the field of Ecumenism', he agreed with the Ukrainian Catholic priest and canonist Archimandrite Victor J. Pospishil that 'there is no discipline of the sacred sciences as

39 Archondonis, 'A Common Code', 45.
40 Ibid.
41 Ibid., 48.
42 Ibid.
43 Ibid., 49.
44 Ibid.
45 Archondonis, 'The Problem of Oikonomia', 46.
46 Bartholomeos Archondonis, 'The Teachings of the Sacred Canons on those who are not in Communion with the Church' 8 *Kanon* (1987) 45–50, at 50.
47 Archondonis, 'The Problem of Oikonomia', 46.
48 Archondonis, 'A Common Code', 51.

amenable to ecumenical endeavors as Canon Law'.[49] This belief, stated explicitly in 1971, has remained strong within His All-Holiness and almost 50 years later, in his 2019 Keynote Address received flesh and bones, when he gave a clear response to the question about how Canon Law can assist the ecumenical movement: through the highlighting of the fundamental principles shared among the various Christian traditions and through the nourishing of their internal legislation with these principles.

The Ecumenical Patriarch did not fail to give even a few concrete examples from within the Orthodox Church on the application of these fundamental principles. With personal satisfaction, Bartholomew mentioned in his Keynote Address two of the documents adopted by the Holy and Great Council of the Orthodox Church, convened under his chairmanship on the island of Crete (Greece) in June 2016, with the active participation of 10 out of the then 14 local Orthodox Churches. In both these two documents explicit reference is made to 'canonical principles'. In the first document about the Orthodox Church and its participation in the ecumenical movement, 'the canonical principles of Orthodox ecclesiology and the canonical criteria of the already established Church Tradition', 'inspired by common fundamental principles of the Gospel', are mentioned as the solid basis on which ecumenical dialogue should be conducted, at least on the part of the Orthodox Church. In the second document about marriage and its impediments, the 'principles of the holy canons' are indicated as precious guides for each local Orthodox Church, when it exercises 'ecclesiastical οἰκονομία in relation to impediments to marriage', such as in the case of a mixed marriage between an Orthodox and a non-Orthodox. In any case, though, His All-Holiness emphasised the unique responsibility prescribed by the Eastern canonical tradition to the Ecumenical Patriarchate, as the guarantor for both safeguarding these fundamental principles at the inter-Orthodox level and their offering on behalf of the Orthodox Church to the inter-Christian dialogue, 'contributing crucially to a dynamic renewal of the canonical consciousness of the Church'.

IV. Conclusion

This last quotation from his 2019 Keynote Address captures in just one sentence the whole essence of His All-Holiness' position on the development of Canon Law. Putting emphasis on the dynamic character of the Church and of its life in this world, the Ecumenical Patriarch constantly treats the sacred canons as a living tradition and he faithfully seeks to

49 Ibid.

renew the practice of the Church on the basis of the fundamental principles he finds in those canons. With remarkable consistency of thought and action, the seed that was planted in his dissertation found fruitful soil and blossomed 50 years later in the field of inter-Christian relations. But this is just one aspect of Bartholomew's canonical legacy.

His breath of vision, his effort to see the canons always in the light of their saving purpose, his refusal to see Canon Law as a discipline in itself, cut off from spirituality, and his attempt to discern the inner coherence of the Church's canonical tradition by following a balanced approach to legalism and antinomianism, have left an indelible mark on modern Orthodox canonical thought. Even more so since all these are not abstract theoretical frameworks elaborated by a scholar in a laboratory, but the living example for the last 32 years of the longest serving Ecumenical Patriarch in history, as Archbishop and Chief-shepherd of the Holy Archdiocese of Constantinople, as President of the Holy and Sacred Synod of the Ecumenical Patriarchate, as President of the Synaxes of the Hierarchy of the Ecumenical Throne, as President of the Synaxes of the Orthodox Primates, as President of the Holy and Great Council of the Orthodox Church, as the spiritual father of all the Eastern Orthodox Christians. In whatever capacity of his 50-year-long hierarchical ministry, His All-Holiness Bartholomew has deservedly earned the title of 'the canonist Patriarch', who 'rightly divides the word' of Christ's truth with an unsurpassed legacy, serving as a model not only for our time, but also for the generations to come.

2 The Principles of Christian Law

Norman Doe

In his Keynote Address at the 24th International Congress of the Society for the Law of the Eastern Churches (Rome, 16 September 2019), Ecumenical Patriarch Bartholomew makes three key propositions, namely that: in the Eastern Orthodox tradition, the ancient and holy canons contain principles of fundamental theological importance to ecclesiology; the work of the Ecumenical Christian Law Panel from 2013–2016, comparing the legal systems of different ecclesial traditions and inducing from them common principles of law, is an important example of ecumenical collaboration in the endeavour to enhance greater visible Christian unity; and the Panel's Statement of Principles of Christian Law, issued in 2016, corrects the historical deficit in the ecumenical enterprise, which hitherto has neglected the potential of church law as a unifying force for global Christianity. What follows elucidates these basic propositions in the canonical thought of Patriarch Bartholomew, contextualises them against the use of principles of law in other church traditions beyond Eastern Orthodoxy, and evaluates their significance in light of the work of the Ecumenical Panel and the launch of its principles of Christian law in 2022 at a workshop of the 11th Assembly of the World Council of Churches held in Germany.

I. The Utility of Principles of Church Law: Ancient and Modern

The concept of canonical principles is an integral part of the legal thought of Patriarch Bartholomew – in the context, that is, of the canons of the Eastern Orthodox Churches. In his 2019 address, the Patriarch observed that:

> In our doctoral dissertation we argued, and in our address at the Society's inaugural Congress we had the opportunity to reiterate, that the ancient canons 'contain the guiding and fundamental principles, on which all legislative work of the Church, created by changing ecclesiastical circumstances, must be based. The Church's legislation

DOI: 10.4324/9781032636740-4

> must always aim: firstly, at the application of the above-mentioned principles in accordance with the special needs of the Church in a given age, and secondly, at the elaboration of these principles in specific appropriate canons'.[1]

Further:

> These canonical principles have a theological content and are fundamental to the Church's ecclesiological self-understanding. They have a living force and contain within themselves the possibility for further development and articulation. They form a dynamic canonical tradition, 'which is the living experience of the whole Church, and not a museum-piece, expressing the demands of each time'.[2]

What the Patriarch sets out so eloquently here is also true for other Christian ecclesial traditions, past and present. These too see church laws as applying or containing principles which themselves are foundational, theological in content, and reflective of a church's self-understanding. First, historically in the Western canonical tradition of the Latin Church, as well as in post-Reformation Anglican jurisprudence, principles of law played a key role in thinking about the nature, sources, and application of church law.

Roman civil law is the starting point for the medieval development of *regulae iuris* in the Latin Church. The last title of Justinian's Digest is *De diversis regulis iuris antiqui.* Its *regulae* are broadly modelled on popular and literary proverbs, influenced by Greek philosophy. A *regula* is 'a brief exposition of an existing state of affairs: not of such a nature that the law is derived from the rule, but the rule is established by the existing law'.[3] In assimilating Roman civil law to the Church and its law, the medieval canon lawyers of the Latin Church also used *regulae* 'to abstract and generalise the decision found in the Roman legal texts and to make explicit their relations with each other'; for example, the great Bernard of Pavia (d. 1213) included a title *de regulis iuris* in his *Compilatio Prima* (1187–1191), and Bertram Bishop of Metz (1181–1212) visualises a *regula* as a 'universal proposition' and *regulae* as *causae cum causa coniunctio* – 'the

1 Bartholomew Archondonis, 'A Common Code for the Orthodox Churches', 1 *Kanon* (1973) 45–53, at 46.

2 See the Address for the footnote reference for the inaugural congress of the Society.

3 R. Pound, 'The maxims of equity – I: of maxims generally', 34 *Harvard Law Review* (1921) 809; P. Stein, *Regulae Iuris: From Juristic Rules to Legal Maxims* (Edinburgh: Edinburgh University Press, 1966).

joining of one principle with another' – and for him *causa* means a principle or *ratio*.[4]

Two landmarks were the *Liber Extra* (or *Gregorian Decretals*, 1234), produced under the direction of Pope Gregory IX (1227–1241), and the *Liber Sextus*, compiled under Pope Boniface VIII (1294–1303) and promulgated in 1298. There are 11 *regulae iuris* at the end of the fifth book of the *Liber Extra* and 88 in the last title of the *Liber Sextus*. Scholars broadly agree about the nature and purposes of these *regulae*. First, they are, variously: moral proverbs; judicial maxims; fundamental laws in the form of axioms; conclusions or deductions, rather than principles of law drawn from constitutions; and general rules or principles serving chiefly for the interpretation of laws. Second, a *regula* may be descriptive or prescriptive. Third, most *regulae* are expressed with a high level of generality: 'No one can be held to the impossible'; 'Time does not heal what was invalid from the beginning'; and 'What one is not permitted to do in his own name, he may not do through another'. It is not surprising, then, that they were used in teaching canon law, both to sum up the law and to resolve contradictions.[5]

After the Reformation, continental civilians and canonists continued to use *regulae iuris*. This 'axiomisation' of law sought a purer and earlier understanding of law, and simplicity in learning the law – students study *regulae* at most European universities.[6] In England, the end of papal jurisdiction and establishment of the Church of England did not result in the abandonment of *regulae iuris* in English ecclesiastical law. For example, Richard Hooker (d. 1600) used 'first principles', 'maxims', and 'axioms' from Roman canon law, as did the church courts. Likewise, Richard Burn (1763) commonly writes of a 'known maxim of the canon law' (e.g. that the church shall not pay tithes to the church). However, the concept of 'maxims' seems to have been displaced in the 19th century with that of 'principles' of church law; for instance, John Henry Blunt (1873) invokes a 'recognised principle' or 'general principle of the canon law'.[7]

Second, more recently, in a bilateral ecumenical context, the Colloquium of Anglican and Roman Catholic Canon Lawyers, uses the

4 P. Stein, op. cit., 131, 144, 145, 147.

5 J. Brundage, *Medieval Canon Law* (London and New York, Longman, 1995) 196–198; A. Meehan, '*Regulae iuris*', *The Catholic Encyclopaedia*, Vol. 12 (New York: R. Appleton, 1911); M.B. Carosi, 'Some notes on the problem of *regulae iuris* in the history of law', 10 *Annuario di emeneutica giuridica* (2005) 305–312.

6 D. van der Merwe, '*Regulae iuris* and the axiomisation of the law and in the sixteenth and early seventeenth centuries', *Journal of South African Law* (1987) 286 at 288.

7 N. Doe and S. Pulleyn, 'The durability of maxims in canon law: from *regulae iuris* to canonical principles', in T. Harris, ed., *Studies in Canon Law and Common Law in Honor of R.H. Helmholz* (Berkeley: The Robbins Collection, 2015) 303–336.

category of principles of law in its work. Set up in 1999, the Colloquium compares the respective laws of the two communions, meets annually, publishes its proceedings, and has addressed such topics as church property, clergy discipline, Christian initiation, authority in the church, orders, ministry, marriage, bishops, and liturgy. Its work is rooted in 'academic rigour, candid exchanges of views, and respectful listening' and its 'agreed principles' have been fed into the ongoing work of the Anglican-Roman Catholic International Commission (ARCIC).[8]

Third, the worldwide Anglican Communion deploys canonical principles to enhance unity between its churches. Based on a comparative study of laws in each autonomous Anglican Church,[9] the Anglican Communion Legal Advisors Network launched at the Lambeth Conference in 2008 *The Principles of Canon Law Common to the Churches of the Anglican Communion* – it has 100 macro-principles and 600 micro-principles in eight parts: church order; Anglican Communion; government; ministry; doctrine and liturgy; rites; church property; and ecumenism.[10] In 2009, the Anglican Consultative Council commended the principles for study, invited comments and requested reports.[11]

As churches continued to legislate since 2008, the principles needed updating. A second version appeared in 2022, a collaboration between the Cardiff Centre for Law and Religion, the Ecclesiastical Law Society, and the Anglican Consultative Council. Online reading groups worldwide suggested revisions; principles were re-drafted and agreed. The new edition was launched at the Lambeth Conference in August 2022. In 2023, the Anglican Consultative Council commended the principles 'for study and use' and encouraged the churches 'to keep their canons under review' in the light of them.[12]

II. The Ecumenical Christian Law Panel

In his Keynote Address 2019, as to 'inter-Christian relations', Bartholomew argues: 'Equality and respect for the canonical traditions of the other are precious values acknowledging the capacity of every participant to discover, understand and experience the truth … through this joint quest', especially 'in their legitimate diversities'. Not only this. First:

8 For 'agreed principles' see e.g. 8th Colloquium, 2007: N. Doe, ed., *The Formation and Ordination of Clergy in Anglican and Roman Catholic Canon Law* (Cardiff: Centre for Law and Religion, 2009) 155.

9 N. Doe, *Canon Law in the Anglican Communion* (Oxford: Oxford University Press, 1998).

10 Published by the Anglican Communion Office, London, 2008.

11 ACC-14, Resolution 14.20.

12 ACC-18, Resolution 3(d).

'Through the comparative study of the various juridical instruments of the Churches ... it is possible to explore critically the extent to which different Christian traditions share common principles in their canons and other instruments of internal governance'. Second, the fruits of this would be: 'to formulate such common principles of Christian law, and to examine the ways in which these ... may contribute to the ecumenical endeavor to enhance fuller visible unity'. Third, he wrote that in March 2019: 'we had the chance to be personally informed ... about the significant canonical work of an Ecumenical Panel' which issued a *Statement of Principles of Christian Law* (2016); he continues: 'These principles were induced from similarities drawn precisely from a comparative study of the regulatory instruments of the participating Christian canonical traditions'.[13] What follows explains the work of the Panel.

In November 2013 an invited Panel of Experts met in Rome. It was convened by Mark Hill QC. Participants attended in their personal capacities, not as representatives of their denominations, and on the basis of their expertise in the church law, church order or church polity, of particular Christian churches: Anglican, Baptist, Catholic, Lutheran, Methodist, Orthodox, Presbyterian, and Reformed. It explored how these churches share common principles in their laws, and how these principles contribute creatively to ecumenism. The Panel was inspired by various 'models': the Patriarch's 1973 article on codifying Eastern Orthodox canon law;[14] the historic use of principles by jurists, the Anglican and Roman Catholic Colloquium of Canon Lawyers, and the Anglican Communion (see above), and studies by Engelhardt, Reuver, Ombres, and Koffeman.[15]

At its first meeting in Rome 2013, the Panel agreed that: (1) there are principles of church law common to the churches studied which can be factually established by empirical observation and comparison; (2) the churches contribute through their laws to these principles; (3) the principles have a theological content and are fundamental to the self-understanding of Christianity; (4) they have a living force and contain the possibility of articulation; and (5) they demonstrate a degree of unity between churches, stimulate common Christian actions, and should feed into global ecumenism to enhance fuller visible unity. Second, the Panel agreed that: church laws exist to serve a church in its mission and witness

13 The statement, he wrote, was 'based on the book *Christian Law: Contemporary Principles*, by Professor Norman Doe' (published by Cambridge University Press, 2013).

14 Ibid., 20, n. 58.

15 H. Engelhardt, 'The lawyer's contribution to the progress of Christian unity', *The Ecumenical Review* (1969) 7–22; M. Reuver, *Faith and Law: Juridical Perspectives for the Ecumenical Movement* (Geneva: World Council of Churches, 2000); R. Ombres, 'Canon law and theology', 14 *Ecclesiastical Law Journal* (2012) 164–194; L.J. Koffeman, *In Order to Serve: An Ecumenical Introduction to Church Polity* (Berlin: LIT, 2014).

to the work of Christ; laws are necessary to facilitate and order churches' activities but cannot encompass all Christian faith and life; laws are the servants of the church and must promote the mission of the church universal; theology shapes law, and law translates theology into norms of conduct; and church laws should conform to the law of God, as revealed in Scripture and by the Holy Spirit. Third, the Panel agreed that a consideration of church law may provide a new medium for the ecumenical enterprise: namely, that law (an element of the self-understanding of churches) should be conceived as an instrument for global ecumenism. Identifying juridical similarities and differences would be of value to ecumenical understanding.[16]

In 2014 the Panel met to discuss how its work might feed into that of the World Council of Churches by means of a response to the World Council of Churches (WCC) Faith and Order Commission Paper No. 214, *The Church: Towards a Common Vision* (2013). At its third meeting in 2015, the Panel achieved three things. First, it finalised its response to *Common Vision*.[17] This showed how comparing church laws: facilitates the articulation of principles of law common to the churches; enables reconciliation of juridical difference in the form of a principle of law; provides a stable ecumenical methodology in using concrete textual data; offers a practical guide for Christian life; and defines achieved communion and opportunities for and limits on future progress. Also: 'Re-imagining ecumenism through law, as applied ecclesiology in … norms of conduct, would advance *Common Vision's* idea that "common action" is "intrinsic to the life and being of the Church"'.[18]

Second, the Panel worked on candidate principles on: church discipline; and church property. In terms of method, the preparatory work asked members to agree, disagree, or agree to differ on the candidate principles. The meeting also gave the opportunity to revise principles over which there was disagreement in order to reconcile differences. The exercise was whether there was legal evidence that the candidate principles appear explicitly or implicitly in the laws of the traditions. Discussion was robust. Of the 50 or so candidate principles circulated, 47 were agreed. The principles, with the Panel response to *Common Vision*, were submitted to WCC in December 2015. Third, the Panel agreed to continue to discern and articulate principles of law on other topics.[19]

16 Panel: Response to *Common Vision* (2013) (December 2015) pp. 3–4.

17 The paper (with changes) was re-produced as N. Doe, 'The Ecumenical Value of Comparative Church Law: Towards the Category of Christian Law', 17 *Ecclesiastical Law Journal* (2015) 135–169.

18 See *Common Vision*, par. 61.

19 Panel: Response (2015) p. 5.

Further candidate principles were circulated.[20] In 2016, the Panel agreed 'A Statement of Principles of Christian Law Common to the Component Churches'.[21] It has ten sections: churches and their laws; the faithful; ordained ministry; church governance; church discipline; doctrine and worship; rites; ecumenism; church property; and church and state relations. Grouping the principles this way, in these sections, is conditioned by the systematisation of laws generally used by the churches from whose laws they are induced. The principles are derived from various sources, including codes of canon law, statutes, constitutions, books of church order, and other policy documents. The juridical values of clarity, conciseness and consistency govern their form and they are cast in a variety of ways, as: permissions, precepts, prohibitions, exhortations, and descriptions – their forms, once more, mirror the laws from which they are induced.[22]

III. The Ecumenical Reception of the Principles of Christian Law

In his Keynote Address 2019, Patriarch Bartholomew expressed 'gladness that a special workshop' was held at the Congress in Rome, at which he delivered his address, which was 'dedicated to this important *Statement*'; he explained the statement was 'being fed into the work of the WCC and its Faith and Order Commission'; and he welcomed how that Commission had in 2017 'established at Geneva a partnership' with the Panel, 'in fulfilment of the acknowledgement by the WCC in 1974 that "church law" should be treated and studied as an instrument of ecumenism'. Importantly, he said that the statement 'is designed to fill the historical canonical deficit in the ecumenical enterprise' as a form of 'juridical ecumenism'.[23]

Indeed, in 2013 and 2014, the Panel noted the WCC's interest in the role of church law in ecumenism, but that this has not been developed. In 1974 the Faith and Order Commission called for discussion of 'church law' on the basis that: 'The churches differ in their order and their constitution'; 'differences in the ... legal systems of the churches have their roots in different confessional traditions'; and these differences concern 'not only the actual order which the churches have, but also the general

20 The candidate principles were those as set out in N. Doe, *Christian Law*, op. cit., Appendix, 387–398.

21 Of the 250 or so candidate principles considered, 230 were accepted (in a revised or added form).

22 For the statement, see N. Doe, ed., *Church Laws and Ecumenism: A New Path for Christian Unity* (Routledge, 2021) 270, Appendix II.

23 He cites N. Doe, 'Juridical Ecumenism', 14 *Ecclesiastical Law Journal* (2012) 195–234).

orientation by which their legislation is inspired'. However, in 1978 the proposal was abandoned: the Director of Faith and Order reported that 'given limited resources available … the study will probably never get very far'; this has led to the view that 'questions and conflicts in these areas have accompanied the ecumenical movement ever since, which confirms the foresight of those earlier initiatives and the need to take them up once again'.[24]

As a result, in 2016 the Panel also decided to seek a meeting in Geneva in 2017 with the Director of the WCC Faith and Order Commission, Dr Odair Mateus. So, in Geneva in November 2017, the Panel presented to Dr Mateus a copy of the *Statement*,[25] the first ecumenical exercise of its type. Dr Mateus recognised the potential unifying force of law as 'an element of the true church'. Dr Ani Ghazaryan Drissi of the Faith and Order Commission Secretariat added that the Panel response to *Common Vision* had been seen, within the Commission process examining this and other responses, as 'unique', 'profound', a 'valuable approach', and an 'alternative path'. Dr Mateus then proposed setting up an 'informal but substantial consultative partnership' between the Panel and the Commission for them to continue working together. The Panel warmly welcomed this – and the partnership was later confirmed by an exchange of letters.[26]

The Panel next met in Rome in November 2018 with Commission members and with new members, Old Catholic and Pentecostal. It agreed that Phase 1 of the work of the Panel was complete (from 2013–2018). It heard how Panel members had already road-tested the statement, at ecumenical events in Uppsala, Cardiff, and Amsterdam in 2018. And so, Phase 2 had already commenced: further events were held in 2019 in London, Melbourne, Sydney, and Oslo. Three days after the Patriarch's address at the Rome Congress, at a private audience in the Apostolic Palace at the Vatican, on 19 September 2019, Pope Francis pronounced, for the first time in papal history, that church law 'is not only an aid to ecumenical dialogue, but also an essential dimension' – more to the point, he said that: 'Canon Law is essential for ecumenical dialogue'; four members of the Panel attended, and presented a copy of the *Statement* to Pope Francis.[27]

Since then, the project has entered Phase 3 – a wider reception at the World Council of Churches, following the publication of a book on the project written by Panel members.[28] At its 2018 meeting, the

24 N. Doe, ed., *Church Laws and Ecumenism*, op cit., 256, Appendix I.

25 M. Hill and N. Doe, 'Principles of Christian Law', 19 *Ecclesiastical Law Journal* (2017) 138–155.

26 N. Doe, ed., *Church Laws and Ecumenism*, op. cit., 24.

27 http://press.vatican.va/content/salastampa/it/bollettino/pubblico/2019/09/19/0714/01466.html

28 N. Doe, ed., *Church Laws and Ecumenism: A New Path for Christian Unity* (Routledge, 2021).

Moderator of the WCC Faith and Order Commission, Susan Durber, had suggested the Panel present its work at the next Assembly of the WCC, its highest governing body which meets every eight years. As a result, on 2 September 2022, at Karlsruhe, Germany, at the 11th Assembly of the WCC, a workshop was held on the *Statement*. I had the privilege to chair it, introduce the background to, models for, and concept underlying the *Statement*. Mark Hill, convenor of the Panel, spoke on the process used by the Panel in drafting the *Statement*. Fr Aetios, Grand Ecclesiarch at the Ecumenical Patriarchate of Constantinople, gave a rich reflection on the value of the *Statement* as a unifying force and instrument for shared ecumenical witness and mission. Participants then discussed its value, sharing their reaction to and experiences of using the *Statement*, from as far afield as India, Australia, the United States, and, in Europe, the Netherlands, Germany, Luxembourg, and Switzerland. They were also keen to be involved in further projects relating to the *Statement*. The workshop then agreed that this 'World Council of Churches workshop commends the *Statement of Principles of Christian Law* for study and use as an essential element of the ecumenical movement'.[29]

IV. Conclusion

The legal thought of Ecumenical Patriarch Bartholomew on canon law, as set out in his Keynote Address at the 24th International Congress of the Society for the Law of the Eastern Churches (2019), articulates three values fundamental to our understanding of canon law: the value of historic canonical principles for ecclesiology; the value as an exercise in ecumenical collaboration of comparing laws of different ecclesial traditions worldwide and inducing from them common principles of law; and the value of an articulation of common principles of Christian law to correct the historic deficit in the ecumenical enterprise, which traditionally has neglected the potential of church law as a unifying force for global Christianity. These are indeed noble, important and practical values – they perpetuate historic uses of principles of church law in other traditions beyond Eastern Orthodoxy; they were put into practice in the work of the Ecumenical Panel on shared principles of church law; and they inspire imaginatively further ecumenical reflection on the *Statement of Principles of Christian Law* (2016) following its launch at a workshop at the 11th Assembly of the World Council of Churches 2022.

29 The Patriarch too welcomed the commendation: www.cardiff.ac.uk/news/view/2674314-cardiff-law-initiative-endorsed-at-the-world-council-of-churches-assembly

Address II

Religion in a Changing Europe

The Role of Religion in a Changing Europe
(London School of Economics, 3 November 2005)

...

Europe, it has often been said, is not simply a geographical area but an idea. What, then, we ask, is the fundamental 'idea' that gives unity to Europe, that constitutes the 'soul' of Europe, and that the European Union is seeking, however imperfectly, to embody?

The answer can be found in a Jewish saying recorded by Martin Buber in his *Tales of the Hasidim*. 'What is the worst thing that the evil urge can achieve?' a rabbi is asked; and he replies, 'To make us forget that we are each the child of a King'.[1] *As* human persons, we are each of us from royal lineage, in the spiritual sense; that is to say, we are each and every one of us *free*. This notion of personal freedom – of the free dignity and integrity of every single human being – lies at the heart of what we mean by the European idea, and it is the primary guiding principle of the European Union. It is precisely from this perspective that we can begin to appreciate the role of religion in Europe, for personal freedom is fundamental likewise to the Christian doctrine of human personhood...

If, however, we are to appreciate the true meaning of this personal freedom, we have to ask further what is meant by 'a person'. Here again, the testimony of the Christian tradition is of decisive significance. Is the human animal merely a political animal, *politikon zōon*, as Aristotle says,[2] or a logical and rational animal, *logikon zōon*, to use the Stoic phrase?[3] Are we no more than an animal that laughs and weeps, as some have thought? Is the human animal to be seen simply in materialistic and economic

1 Martin Buber, *Tales of the Hasidim: The Early Masters* (New York: Schocken Books, 1968) 282.

2 Aristotle, *Politics* I.I.9 (1253a).

3 *Stoicorum Veterum Fragmenta*, ed., H. von Arnim, Ill (1903) 95, §390.

DOI: 10.4324/9781032636740-5

terms, as a consumer? Such, unfortunately, is exactly the approach of many citizens today within the European Union: they think almost exclusively of what they can get out of the Union in terms of material advantages, not of what they can contribute on a spiritual level, and that is perhaps the chief reason why the European Union at present is passing through such a severe crisis.

Against this concept of the person as merely an economic entity, a consumer, Christianity insists that as human beings we are *zōon theoumenon*, to use the words of Sr. Gregory Nazianzus[4] – 'an animal that is called to be deified', that is invited to share in God's glory and to become a 'partaker of the divine nature' (2 Pet. 1.4,). The most important fact about our humanness is our transcendent dimension: we are formed in the image of God (Gen. 1.26). We are endowed, that is to say, with God-consciousness, and so we are capable of prayer. We have the capacity to offer the world back to God in thanksgiving, and it is only in this act of offering that we become genuinely human and truly free.

We do not expect all this to be seated explicitly in the Constitution of the European Union; for the Constitution is a legal document, not a theological treatise. But it is our hope that, implicitly if not explicitly, the foundational document of the European Union will at least be open to such an interpretation. We trust that full recognition will be given to the fact that man does not live by bread alone.

Hitherto, we have spoken of 'personal freedom', but it also needs to be said that our freedom is not only personal but interpersonal. As human beings, we cannot be genuinely free in isolation, repudiating our relationship with our fellow humans. We can be genuinely free only if we form part of a community of other free persons. Freedom is not solitary but social. We are free only if we become a *prosopon* – to use the Greek word for 'person', which means literally 'face' or 'countenance' – only if we turn toward others, looking into their eyes and allowing them to look into ours. To turn away, to refuse to share, is to forfeit liberty.

This indeed is specifically what is implied by the Christian doctrine of God. According to the teaching of the Greek Fathers, 'in the image of God' means primarily 'in the image of Christ'; to be human is to be Christlike, for Christ is the supreme model of what it is to be a person. But the phrase 'in the image of God' means also 'in the image of God the Trinity'. As Christians, we believe in a God who is not only one but one-in-three. The Christian God is not merely personal but also interpersonal; God is not just a unit but a union. As Trinity, God is not simply the Monad, unique, self-sufficient. God is the Triad of Father, Son, and Holy Spirit, the three divine persons united to one another in the

4 *Oration* 38.II.

unceasing movement of mutual love that the Greek patristic tradition terms 'coinherence' or 'co-indwelling' (*perichoresis*). God is communion (*koinonia*) … As Metropolitan John (Zizioulas) of Pergamon expresses it: 'The being of God is a relational being: without the concept of communion it would not be possible to speak of the being of God'.[5]

Now, if as humans we are formed in the image of the Trinity, then it follows that everything that has just been said about God should be applied also to humankind … – this we seek to do not only on the level of our interior life of prayer, not only within the immediate circle of our family and friends, but also more broadly on an economic and political level. Our social programme is the doctrine of the Trinity. Every form of community – the workplace, the school, the city, the nation, even the European Union – has as its vocation to become, each in its own way, a living icon of the Trinity. Nations are called to be transparent to one another, just as the three persons of the Trinity are transparent to one another. Such is the role of religion in a changing Europe.

To some of you, we fear, that what we have just been saying about the imitation of God the Trinity may appear remote, unreal, and overidealistic. Of course, we do not expect such language to be used in the legal formulations and the official documents of the European Union. Yet such are the decisive inner convictions that inspire our commitment as Christians to a united Europe.

…

5 John D. Zizioulas. *Being as Communion: Studies in Personhood and the Church* (Crestwood, NY: St. Vladimir's, Seminary Press, 1985) 17.

3 The European Union and Religion

Frank Cranmer

In 2005, Ecumenical Patriarch Bartholomew gave an address at the London School of Economics at the invitation of the London Hellenic Society on 'The Role of Religion in a Changing Europe' in which he asked, 'In what particular ways is Europe undergoing change?' and noted that two features which came immediately to mind were multiculturalism and increasing secularisation.[1] He returned to the theme three years later in an address to the European Parliament (EP). Reflecting on that occasion on the statement in Decision No 1983/2006 of the Parliament and the Council on the European Year of Intercultural Dialogue that dialogue between citizens was at the heart of the European project, his principal message was that such dialogue was at the very root of what it was to be a human being. Without it, the differences in the human family were reduced to objectifications of the 'other', leading to what he described as the terrible effects of human fragmentation: abuse, conflict, and persecution. Tribalism, fundamentalism, and extreme nationalism without regard to the rights of others all contributed to 'a list of atrocities that give pause to our claims of being civilised in the first place'.[2]

Almost 20 years on, the issues which the Patriarch raised then have, if anything, become of even greater relevance as Europe has become at once more multicultural/multi-faith and more overtly secularist – and at a time when, in a manifestation of the extreme nationalism that he condemned so forthrightly, the Russian Federation, the nation with by far the largest Orthodox population, is waging war on its Orthodox neighbour Ukraine.

1 'The role of religion in a changing Europe: address at the London School of Economics at the invitation of London Hellenic Society, November 3, 2005', in J. Chryssavgis, ed., *In the World, Yet Not of the World: Social and Global Initiatives of Ecumenical Patriarch Bartholomew* (New York: Fordham UP, 2010) 109–120.

2 'Address of His All-Holiness Ecumenical Patriarch Bartholomew to the Plenary Assembly of the European Parliament' (Brussels, 24 September 2008).

DOI: 10.4324/9781032636740-6

I. Religion and the European Institutions

It should be said at the outset that in terms of their relationship with 'religion', it is only with difficulty that the European Union (EU) and the Council of Europe (CoE, of which all European countries apart from Belarus, the Russian Federation, and the Vatican are members) can be considered separately because their respective treaty provisions are inextricably intertwined. Together with the third major European institution – the Organization for Security and Co-operation in Europe (OSCE) – all three acknowledge the importance of religion within European history and culture; and their core documents, the EU Charter of Fundamental Rights (CFR), the CoE European Convention on Human Rights (ECHR) and the Conference on Security and Co-operation in Europe Final Act (CSCEFA), give formal recognition to freedom of thought, conscience and religion.[3]

Though they are not identical, both Article 9 ECHR and Article 10 CFR as first agreed in Nice in 2000 affirm 'the right to freedom of thought, conscience and religion' in very similar terms – the former states:

> Everyone has the right to freedom of thought, conscience and religion; this right includes freedom to change his religion or belief and freedom, either alone or in community with others and in public or private, to manifest his religion or belief, in worship, teaching, practice and observance.

Article 9 ECHR goes on to state that the freedom to manifest

> shall be subject only to such limitations as are prescribed by law and are necessary in a democratic society in the interests of public safety, for the protection of public order, health or morals, or for the protection of the rights and freedoms of others,

while Article 10 CFR declares that 'The right to conscientious objection is recognised, in accordance with the national laws governing the exercise of this right'.

The Preamble to the current text of the CFR:

> reaffirms, with due regard for the powers and tasks of the Union and for the principle of subsidiarity, the rights as they result, in particular, from the constitutional traditions and international obligations

3 Article 9 ECHR, Article 10 CFR, Article VII CSCEFA.

> common to the Member States, the European Convention for the Protection of Human Rights and Fundamental Freedoms, the Social Charters adopted by the Union and by the Council of Europe and the case-law of the Court of Justice of the European Union and of the European Court of Human Rights.[4]

Furthermore, Article 6.3 of the Treaty on the European Union (TEU) declares that fundamental rights *as guaranteed by the ECHR* 'shall constitute general principles of the Union's law'.

Accordingly, the European Union's Court of Justice (CJEU) takes careful note of the decisions of the European Court of Human Rights (ECtHR): it has declared that the ECHR has special significance,[5] and has held that, where Charter rights correspond to those guaranteed by the ECHR, 'their meaning and scope are to be the same as those in the ECHR'.[6] In what follows, therefore, it should be remembered that European law on both religion and on human rights more generally must be understood both from the perspective of the European Union and within the wider context of the ECHR and the jurisprudence of Strasbourg.

II. A 'Soul for Europe'?

In his address at the LSE, the Ecumenical Patriarch reminded his listeners that 'the founding fathers of the European Union, such as Konrad Adenauer and Alcide de Gasperi, were profoundly Christian in their vision of a unified Europe'[7] – to whom he might well have added Robert Schuman, a devout Roman Catholic who in 2021 was declared a 'Servant of God' by Pope Francis and given the title 'Venerable' as the first step towards canonisation.[8] Whatever their vision, however, the institutional relationships between 'religion' and the individual EU Member States vary enormously: from Malta, for example (where Article 2 of the Constitution declares that 'The religion of Malta is the Roman Catholic Apostolic Religion' and 'The authorities of the Roman Catholic Apostolic Church have the duty and the right to teach which principles are right and which are wrong') to stoutly secularist and separationist France (which

4 2012/C 326/02.
5 *Akrich v Secretary of State for the Home Department* [2003] EUECJ C-109/01.
6 *J McB v L E* [2010] EUECJ C-400/10 at para [53].
7 Chryssavgis, 112.
8 Anon, 'Robert Schuman, father of European unity, on path to sainthood' (*Vatican News*, 19 June 2021).

Article I of the Constitution declares to be 'une République indivisible, *laïque*, démocratique et sociale').

Given the absence of national consensus about relations between religion and the state, it is hardly surprising that the institutional relationship between the European Union itself and 'religion' in the wider sense has long been a matter of debate. In a speech to representatives of the European Churches in 1992, Commission President Jacques Delors argued that the Union would not succeed solely through legal expertise or economic know-how:

> If in the next ten years we haven't managed to give a soul to Europe, to give a spirituality and meaning, the game will be up … This is why I want to revive the intellectual and spiritual debate on Europe. I invite the Churches to participate actively in it. We don't want to control it; it is a democratic discussion, not to be monopolised by technocrats … We must find a way of involving the Churches.[9]

The issue came to the fore once more in 2002 when the EU Treaty was, in effect, being renegotiated within the European Convention chaired by Valéry Giscard d'Estaing. One of the issues under consideration was whether there was to be any mention of the religious heritage of the Union in the Preamble to what was to become the European Union Reform Treaty 2007 (EURT).

In the course of that renegotiation, His All-Holiness suggested to his audience at the LSE that the European Union was 'passing through a time of crisis' and that its political leaders had to ask themselves why so many citizens were strongly hostile to the proposed Constitutional Treaty. Perhaps ironically in view of recent events, he cited the rapid growth of Orthodoxy in the former Soviet Union and Ukraine as evidence of Christianity's continued relevance and expressed disappointment that the proposed Treaty made no explicit reference to its contribution to the European heritage.[10]

In his view, the 'soul' of Europe that the European Union was seeking to embody, however imperfectly, had to be based on the twin notions of personal freedom – 'the free dignity and integrity of every single human being' – and personhood 'formed in the image of God', and he expressed

9 J. Krause, *A Soul for Europe? Contributions of European Churches to the Forum of the Convention on the Future of Europe* (Unpublished Master's Thesis, Helsinki University 1.1, 2007), available at <https://helda.helsinki.fi/bitstream/handle/10138/21712/asoulfor.pdf?sequence>: L. Hogebrink, *Europe's Heart and Soul: Jacques Delors' Appeal to the Churches* (Brussels: Conference of European Churches, 2015) 16.

10 Chryssavgis, 111–112.

the hope that 'implicitly if not explicitly, the foundational document of the EU will at least be open to such an interpretation'.[11] He also referred to the growth in the Muslim population across Europe and concluded, 'Surely we should see this not as a threat but as an opportunity',[12] emphasising the need for national identities to be lived out within a pluralistic and multicultural context. Since then, the Muslim population has continued to grow, probably as much because of its age profile as because of immigration, and as the population of Europe becomes ever more religiously and ethnically diverse, his message becomes ever more relevant.

In the event, the Giscard Convention concluded that it was simply too difficult for the European Union *as an institution* to attempt to formulate an overall statement on religion, and the EURT as finally agreed inserted the following into the Preamble of the Treaty on the European Union (TEU) as the second recital:

> DRAWING INSPIRATION from the cultural, religious and humanist inheritance of Europe, from which have developed the universal values of the inviolable and inalienable rights of the human person, freedom, democracy, equality and the rule of law.

Possibly for the same reasons, the EURT avoided specifying exactly *which* spiritual or religious heritage was inspirational, with the result that Article 2 of the TEU declares the Union to be

> founded on the values of respect for human dignity, freedom, democracy, equality, the rule of law and respect for human rights, including the rights of persons belonging to minorities. These values are common to the Member States in a society in which pluralism, non-discrimination, tolerance, justice, solidarity and equality between women and men prevail.

Looking back in 2008, Giscard concluded that though the debate had been inconclusive, Europe until the 18th century had nevertheless been Christian: 'It's not a value judgment, it's not saying it's good or bad. It's just how it is'.[13] Nor was that anything new: the Preamble to the CFR of 2000 had already declared that 'Conscious of its spiritual and moral heritage', the Union was founded on the indivisible, universal val-

11 Chryssavgis, 115–116.
12 Chryssavgis, 110.
13 H. Bribosia, 'Transcription of the interview with Valéry Giscard d'Estaing (Paris, 17 November 2008)' 17, Luxembourg: CVCE.EU, <www.cvce.eu/content/publication/2011/3/3/b3e39520-70b9-4bda-9ad2-02d83be29649/publishable_en.pdf>

ues of human dignity, freedom, equality and solidarity, and the Seventh Framework Programme Directive, Council Decision (EC) 1982/2006, had already recognised 'religions' as one 'building element' of European multicultural identity and heritage.

III. Religion and Subsidiarity

Article 17 of the consolidated 2012 text of the Treaty on the Functioning of the European Union (TFEU), as amended by the EURT, recognises both 'the cultural, religious and humanist inheritance of Europe' and the status under *national* law of churches, religious associations/communities, and philosophical and non-confessional organisations, and commits the Union to 'an open, transparent and regular dialogue' with them. So far as the Christian Churches are concerned, that dialogue is conducted for the Churches in communion with Rome by the Commission of the Bishops' Conferences of the European Union (COMECE) and for the Churches of the Orthodox, Protestant, and Anglican traditions by the Conference of European Churches (CEC). So far as possible, they work together – so, for example, their Presidents issued a joint statement at the launch of the Conference on the Future of Europe on Europe Day 2021 which committed their institutions to 'strengthening our common European values, combating climate change and preserving the creation, and developing migration policies based on respect for human rights and the human dignity of everyone'.[14] The Jewish and Muslim faiths and the Quakers also have full-time representation in Brussels.

The principle of subsidiarity as recognised in the CFR first emerged in the Preamble to the Treaty on the European Union as signed in Maastricht in 1992. Though it is not unlike the margin of appreciation afforded to states parties by the ECtHR, the two are by no means identical: subsidiarity applies to the organs of the European Union *generally* in areas that do not fall within its exclusive competence, not merely to the CJEU. Under Article 5(3) of the TEU

> the Union shall act only if and in so far as the objectives of the proposed action cannot be sufficiently achieved by the Member States, either at central level or at regional and local level, but can rather, by reason of the scale or effects of the proposed action, be better achieved at Union level.

14 J-C. Hollerich and C. Krieger, 'COMECE and CEC applaud the launch of the Conference on the Future of Europe' (Brussels, COMECE 7 May 2021).

The regulation of religion is not expressly listed among the European Union's competences, though subjects associated with religion, such as culture and education, are listed explicitly in, for example, Article 6 TFEU, and both it and the CFR recognise the right of Member States to determine the legal position of domestic religious organisations over a wide range of issues. So, for example, the European Union recognises that 'the special status granted to Mount Athos, as guaranteed by Article 105 of the Hellenic Constitution, is justified exclusively on grounds of a spiritual and religious nature',[15] while the CJEU has upheld the validity of moral and religious factors in national decision-making on the regulation of gambling.[16] Though the CJEU rejected the United Kingdom's attempt to have Directive 93/104/EC on working time annulled, it did annul the second sentence of Article 5, which would have made Sunday the Europe-wide day of rest.[17]

The principle of subsidiarity is not, however, absolute. National religious affairs are primarily matters for national governments and the European Union will normally respect the status of religious organisations under national laws; nevertheless, it may decide on matters falling within its competence even if they have indirect religious implications for national jurisdictions. So, for example, when the original Treaty of Rome was being drafted in the early 1950s, no-one would have imagined that society would one day cease to treat same-sex relationships with disapproval – and in many cases with criminal sanctions. By 2018, however, the CJEU's Grand Chamber was prepared to rule that member states that did not themselves recognise same-sex marriage had nevertheless to recognise same-sex marriages concluded in other member states for the purposes of rights of residence.[18]

Furthermore, there is an inevitable tension between subsidiarity and commonality. As His All Holiness pointed out, nations in the contemporary world are no longer self-sufficient but interdependent, and although each bears its own distinct and valuable characteristics, 'national identity has today to be lived out within a pluralistic and multicultural context'.[19]

15 *Documents concerning the accession of the Hellenic Republic to the European Communities, Final Act, Joint Declaration concerning Mount Athos*, 11979H/AFI/DCL/04.

16 *HM Customs and Excise v Gerhart Schindler and Jorg Schindler* [1994] EUECJ C-275/92.

17 *United Kingdom of Great Britain and Northern Ireland v Council of the European Union* [1996] EUECJ C-84/94.

18 *Coman and Others* [2018] EUECJ C-673/16.

19 Chryssavgis, 110.

IV. Personal and Religious Freedom and Non-Discrimination

In his 2005 address, Ecumenical Patriarch Bartholomew argued that personal freedom and the dignity and integrity of every human being lay at the heart of 'the European idea' and was the European Union's primary guiding principle.[20] The CJEU has declared that 'the Community legal order undeniably strives to ensure respect for human dignity as a general principle of law'[21] and that non-discrimination is a fundamental principle of EU law,[22] while Article 21 CFR prohibits discrimination 'on any ground', including 'religion or belief, political or other opinion'. In applying the law, however, the institutions of the European Union are required to strike a fair balance between the rights of religious communities to regulate their internal proceedings and the right of individuals not to be unfairly discriminated against.

So, for example, Directive (EC) 93/104 – the Working Time Directive – allows derogations from prescribed requirements for workers officiating in religious ceremonies provided there is proper regard for health and safety, while Directive (EC) 2000/78 – the Equal Treatment Directive – prohibits direct and indirect discrimination on grounds of religion or belief. Article 4(2) of Directive (EC) 2000/78 permits religious discrimination for 'occupational activities within churches and other public or private organisations the ethos of which is based on religion or belief' where the nature or context of those activities means that religion or belief is 'a genuine, legitimate and justified occupational requirement' – but the CJEU has ruled that where a religious organisation imposes a religious requirement for employment it must be a genuine one.[23] So, for example, the CJEU held that remarriage after divorce without a prior annulment was not a justifiable ground for dismissing a Head of Department of a Roman Catholic hospital because it did not appear to be necessary for the promotion of the hospital's ethos – and similar positions in the hospital were held by non-Catholics who were not subject to the same discipline.[24]

On the issue of religious symbols in the workplace, the Court has been rather more nuanced. In *Achbita*, it ruled that a general internal rule of a private undertaking prohibiting the visible wearing of any political, philosophical or religious sign in the workplace did not constitute

20 Chryssavgis, 115.

21 *Omega Spielhallen* [2004] EUECJ C-36/02 at [34].

22 *Mangold v Helm* [2005] EUECJ C-144/04.

23 *Vera Egenberger v Evangelisches Werk für Diakonie und Entwicklung eV* [2018] EUECJ C-414/16.

24 *IR* [2018] EUECJ C-68/17.

direct discrimination based on religion or belief within the meaning of the Equal Treatment Directive 2000/78,[25] but that it might constitute *indirect* discrimination if it put persons of a particular religion or belief at a particular disadvantage unless it was objectively justified by a legitimate aim; it suggested that the pursuit by an employer of a policy of political, philosophical and religious neutrality in its relations with its customers could be a legitimate aim so long as the means of achieving it were appropriate and necessary.[26] On the same day, however, it concluded in *Bougnaoui* that the willingness of an employer to take account of the wishes of a customer who did not wish to have that employer's services provided by a worker wearing an Islamic headscarf could not be considered a genuine and determining occupational requirement under the Directive.[27]

V. Cooperation with Faith Communities

Under Article 17.3 TFEU, 'the Union shall maintain an open, transparent, and regular dialogue with ... churches and organisations'. Cooperation may be justified on the basis of the particular expertise of religious bodies in, for example, moral and social affairs – but it may also represent a pragmatic response to the fact that religions have simply refused to accept being marginalised by the separation of the state and religion. Moreover, the principle merely articulates existing EU practices and procedures: Decision (EC) 2006/971 on Specific Programme Cooperation, for example, accepts that 'appreciation and understanding of differences between value systems of different religions or ethnic minority groups lay foundations for positive attitudes'.

The obligation under the Lisbon Treaty to cooperate in dialogue with religions that became Article 17.3 TFEU goes beyond the constitutional laws of member states – and sometimes, indeed, beyond the reach of the European Union. In spite of the fact that it did not originate from the organs of the European Union, the Council of Europe's White Paper, *Living Together as Equals in Dignity* CM (2008) has given rise to an annual dialogue between representatives of faith groups and life-stances and the European Parliament (*not*, it should be noted, the Parliamentary Assembly of the CoE), of which the most recent was held in January 2023. The Parliament nominates a member of its Presidency to be

25 That position was subsequently confirmed in *WABE v MH Müller Handels GmbH* [2021] EUECJ C-804/18.

26 *Achbita & Anor v G4S Secure Solutions NV* [2017] EUECJ C-157/15 at [44].

27 *Bougnaoui and ADDH* [2017] EUECJ C-188/15 at [42].

responsible for the Parliament's implementation of Article 17 TFEU: the current nominee is Othmar Karas, First Vice-President.

VI. Conclusion: 'A Happy Concord'?

One must never assume that the principles of human dignity and integrity are simply a given: the global evidence for their non-observance is simply too great to support such a view. Even liberal European democracies are not immune from sporadic bouts of illiberalism, as witnessed in the publication by the UK Government of its Illegal Migration Bill on 7 March 2023, which instead of the usual declaration of legislative compatibility with the ECHR begins with a statement on the face of the Bill that the Home Secretary was 'unable to make a statement that, in my view, the provisions of the Illegal Migration Bill are compatible with the Convention rights, but the Government nevertheless wishes the House to proceed with the Bill'.

In a similar vein, the Polish Government has been in dispute with the European Union since 2020 over its creation of a disciplinary chamber for its judges at the Supreme Court. In 2021, the CJEU declared that its creation breached Poland's obligations under the second subparagraph of Article 19(1) TEU to provide remedies sufficient to ensure effective legal protection in the fields covered by Union law, and Poland was ordered to pay a daily fine of 1 million euros until such time as it complied with the order of the Court or, if it failed to do so, until the date of delivery of the final judgement.[28]

The contribution of His All-Holiness to the debate about the role of religion in the future of Europe has therefore been very significant, not just by virtue of his position as Ecumenical Patriarch but because of his repeated insistence that personal freedom – the free dignity and integrity of every human being – is fundamental both to the 'European idea' and the guiding principles of the European Union and, equally, to the Christian doctrine of human personhood.[29] He has also emphasised the need for mutual respect and cooperation between the secular authorities and faith communities, suggesting that the paradigm for the relationship between the state and religion should be 'a happy concord' and concluding that 'Freedom, respect, and the dignity and integrity of each human person are fundamental to our vision of a united Europe'.[30]

28 *Commission v Poland* [2021] EUECJ C-791/19, *Commission v Poland (Order)* [2021] EUECJ C-204/21 CO, *Commission v Poland* [2022] EUECJ C-204/21.

29 Chryssavgis, 115.

30 Chryssavgis, 120.

The relationship between the European Union and religion is both complex and multifaceted, as evidenced by the various institutional relationships between religion and the individual Member States. Though some of the founding fathers of the European Union were devout Christians, and though Christianity has played a significant role in Europe's cultural and political heritage, in order to achieve that 'happy concord' the European institutions must strike a proper balance between the rights of religious communities to regulate their internal proceedings and the rights of individuals not to be unfairly discriminated against – a task that becomes ever more important as Europe becomes ever more multicultural, secular, and religiously and ethnically diverse.

Europe, declared Ecumenical Patriarch Bartholomew in an address to the College of Europe in 2019,

> is a great experiment of solidarity on a continent that during the last century experienced the two most bloody and terrible wars in the history of humanity. It is a project of peaceful coexistence, freedom, justice and respect of human rights and of pluralism.[31]

His contribution to that project cannot be overestimated.

31 'Address by His All-Holiness Ecumenical Patriarch Bartholomew "The Role of the Churches in Today's Europe"' (College of Europe, Bruges 11 November 2019) <www.coleurope.eu/sites/default/files/speech-files/speech_patriarch_bartholomeus.pdf?download=1>

4 The States of Europe and Religion

Miguel Rodríguez Blanco

At the dawn of the 21st century, at a time when terrorist attacks had shaken the Western world and state policies had shifted from the paradigm of freedom to that of security,[1] Ecumenical Patriarch Bartholomew gave an address at the London School of Economics entitled 'The Role of Religion in a Changing Europe'.[2] Despite the geopolitical and social changes that have taken place in the almost two decades since his lecture, delivered in November 2005, the reflections it contains are equally relevant today. The diagnosis he makes of the characteristics that define European societies in terms of religion – multiculturalism and secularisation – and the proposals he makes for harmonious and peaceful coexistence between all people who make up society are wholly valid for our time.

Reading the text, one gets the impression that the political situation, and social challenges faced, have hardly changed. However, the changes which European societies have undergone are evident and structural. Suffice it to cite the deepening of the defining features of globalisation, the advance in technological development in fields such as artificial intelligence, the constant increase in migratory flows – in particular, the arrival of refugees on European soil – the COVID-19 pandemic, or the challenges to security and peaceful coexistence arising from terrorist actions and armed conflicts. The value of the Ecumenical Patriarch's reflections lies in his ability to grasp reality, anticipate future developments, and identify present and future challenges. He does not take a snapshot of a precise moment, but rather provides a description rooted in history in order to project itself into the future. Past, present and future are intertwined in a clear-sighted discourse.

1 S. Ferrari, 'Religion and Security in Europe After September 11: A Gloomy Perspective?', 1 *Quaderni di diritto e politica ecclesiastica* (2005) 161–184.

2 'The role of religion in a changing Europe: address at the London School of Economics at the invitation of London Hellenic Society, November 3, 2005', in J. Chryssavgis, ed., *In the World, yet not of the World: Social and Global Initiatives of Ecumenical Patriarch Bartholomew* (New York: Fordham University Press, 2010) 109–120.

DOI: 10.4324/9781032636740-7

In this global vision of Europe, which forms the basis of his lecture, he reflects on the role of religion and the way in which civil authorities should relate to religious groups present in society. He emphasises the 'soul' of Europe, its spiritual heritage, the role of Christianity in the building of European democracies, religion as a feature of the identity of both individuals and states, and a strong defence of the freedom and dignity of every human being. As His All-Holiness explains, the way states choose to relate to religious groups is deeply embedded in historical experiences whose lessons inform current policies. At the same time, the model chosen is not an innocuous one, but constitutes a valuable tool with which to contribute to the freedom, dignity and integrity of every human being, understood as a social being in relationship with others.

Based on Ecumenical Patriarch Bartholomew's vision of the relationship between the state and religions, this chapter aims to show the importance and wisdom of his contributions. To this end, reference will first be made to the models of relations between religious denominations and states that exist in Europe (I). Next, the absence of a common European model will be highlighted (II), although the plurality of attitudes towards religion does not prevent the identification of features common to the different models (III). Another factor on which this chapter dwells is the permanent evolution of the models and their contribution to the objective of guaranteeing peaceful coexistence in a framework of freedom (IV).

I. Models of State–Religion Relations in Europe

In his address, the Ecumenical Patriarch refers to three systems of relationship between the state and organised religions:

> There is first the *confessional* system, whereby the state gives official recognition to one particular religion or church. Second, there is the *non-confessional* system, whereby the state is separated from religion and assumes an attitude of neutrality toward all expressions of religious belief and practice. In the third place, the state is officially *atheist*.
>
> Within the European Union, only the first two systems exist; there is within it no example of a state that is officially atheist.[3]

The classifications of models of Church–State relations are the result of theoretical elaborations. This explains why there are variations from one author to another and why there is no single formulation. The most

3 Chryssavgis, 118.

common classification in recent legal literature refers to the following three models: state church systems, separation systems and hybrid or cooperation systems.[4] Among the current models, the system of *atheism*, which was abandoned in Europe after the fall of the Berlin Wall, the Balkan conflict and the demise of the Soviet Union, is not usually mentioned. Within the state church systems, a distinction must be made between Protestant (established churches or state churches), Catholic (confessional states), and Orthodox (predominant churches) models.[5]

All these categories have relative value and their practical usefulness from a legal point of view is limited. This explains the plurality of terms used to refer to the models.[6] They are not precise legal concepts. They are notions that serve above all to describe the main features of each state and to classify countries according to their predominant characteristics and historical tradition. The classification of a given state as separatist, confessional or cooperative does not have precise and uniform legal consequences that are common to all countries that fall into this category. The legal treatment of religion in each national legal system has many nuances and peculiarities that are the result of historical developments, political situations and the social demands of each moment.

The first reason for the limited practical usefulness of the classification of the systems of Church–State relations is that none of them exists in a pure state, in a perfect form, in practice. Ecumenical Patriarch Bartholomew warns of this in the following words:

> Both in the confessional and the non-confessional systems, there are of course many variations in detail. Even where the non-confessional system prevails, it is usually accepted that religion cannot be simply a private matter for each citizen but that it has implications for the public life of the state, implications that may be recognised on the legal level. In some non-confessional states, for example, religious bodies continue to play an official role in the educational system. Thus, even in non-confessional countries, usually there is no attempt to establish a *total* separation between religion and the state.[7]

4 N. Doe, *Law and Religion in Europe* (Oxford: Oxford University Press, 2011) 28–39.

5 'Church-State relations in the world of Eastern Orthodoxy are collectively quite distinctive, relative to both Catholic and Protestant patters': J. Madeley, 'A Framework for the Comparative Analysis of Church-State Relations in Europe', in 26:1 *West European Politics* (2003) 23–50, at 26.

6 Sometimes referred to as the cooperative model, establishment model and endorsement model. See J.H.H. Weiler, 'Freedom of Religion and Freedom from Religion: The European Model', in 65:2 *Maine Law Review* (2013) 760.

7 Chryssavgis, 119.

In many European states, defining elements of each of the different models mentioned above coexist. Thus, while the state grants a particular legal status to a specific religious group, it implements initiatives of cooperation with various religious denominations and adopts policies of separation that limit the public manifestation of religious beliefs.

The second reason for the relative value of theoretical-descriptive categories is the influence or weight of history. The models are the result of a particular evolution which, on many occasions, is linked to the birth and consolidation of each state. Religion has historically played a very important role as a factor of national identity, a role that is maintained, albeit to a lesser extent, today.[8] The very configuration of the fundamental right to religious freedom in Europe has its roots in the Peace of Augsburg (1555) and the Peace of Westphalia (1648), from which emanates a notion of religious tolerance as a guarantee of peaceful coexistence and respect for the beliefs of all people, which would be the seed of modern freedom of belief.

A good example of this is the French case, a typical separatist model. The 1905 Law of Separation prohibits public funding of religious denominations and the teaching of religion is excluded from schools. However, religious assistance is provided for in public establishments (army, hospitals, prisons, schools) and the state covers the costs of chaplaincies. At the same time, tax regulations provide for tax exemptions for real estate used for religious purposes and patronage regulations encourage donations to religious groups. In addition, the Concordat of 1801 is still in force in Alsace and Moselle, where a model of state-recognised religions is maintained.[9]

II. The Absence of a Single European Model

The confluence of historical circumstances with national identity elements explains the statement that 'there are many European models for dealing with religion in legal terms'.[10] Judge Tulkens has referred to this diversity in the following terms:

8 J. Madeley, 'A Framework for the Comparative Analysis of Church-State Relations in Europe', op. cit., 23–50.

9 For a general overview of the French model, see F. Messner, 'State and Church in France', in G. Robbers, ed., *State and Church in the European Union* (Baden-Baden: Nomos, 2019) 213–237.

10 A. Ferrari, 'Human Rights and the Osmosis between Secular and Religious Legal Systems. The Post- modern European Right to Freedom of Religion through the Prism of the Islamic Veil', in J. Marko, M. Lakitsch, W. Weirer, F. Winter, and K. Wonisch, eds., *Religious Diversity, State, and Law: National, Transnational and International Challenges* (Leiden/Boston: Brill Nijhoff, 2022) 25.

> As far as religion–State relations are concerned, we are therefore faced in Europe with many different legal models: from one extreme (confusion of Church and State with a national Church in Great Britain, Denmark and Greece) to the other (complete or moderate separation of the Church from State under the concept of secularism in Turkey, of *laïcité* in France or neutrality in Belgium), all of them being highly ambiguous terms.[11]

This plurality of legal approaches to religion has led the European Union to respect and not prejudge the status under national law of churches and religious associations or communities in the Member States, under Article 17(1) of the Treaty on the Functioning of the European Union (TFEU). This formulation first appeared as a Declaration annexed to the 1997 Treaty of Amsterdam and is now incorporated at the highest normative level in EU law.

It is clear from its content that the European Union refrains from imposing a common model of relations between the state and religions. Moreover, it refrains from making a value judgement on which system is more appropriate, since it *respects* and *does not prejudge*. This does not mean that the European Union renounces regulating issues relating to religion, as it has competence over a number of matters where religious beliefs or the actions of confessional groups are relevant. The European Union's commitment to the protection of human rights and to the prohibition of discrimination entails that it protects the freedom of the individual to choose his or her beliefs, to manifest them in private and in public and to act in accordance with them. Similarly, the prohibition of both direct and indirect discrimination on grounds of religion is a general principle which applies to various areas of EU law, including employment and occupation.

The Court of Justice of the European Union has explained that while Article 17(1) TFEU expresses the *neutrality* of the European Union towards the organisation by the Member States of their relations with churches and religious associations and communities, that provision cannot be relied upon in order to exclude from the scope of EU law altogether the activity of churches or religious associations and communities where that activity consists in actions under the competence of the European Union.[12] The opinion of Advocate General Emiliou delivered on 7 July 2022 clearly expresses the scope of the words *respect* and not

11 F. Tulkens, 'The European Convention on Human Rights and Church-State Relations: Pluralism vs. Pluralism', 30(6) *Cardozo Law Review* (2009) 2577.

12 *Freikirche der Siebenten-Tags-Adventisten in Deutschland KdöR* (C-372/21) 2 February 2023, paragraph 19.

prejudge, which is far from an incompetence of the European Union in the matter:

> it does not follow from Article 17(1) TFEU that relations between religious communities and a Member State are completely shielded from any review of compliance with EU law 'whatever the circumstances'. In other words, Article 17(1) TFEU cannot be considered … akin to a 'block exemption' for any matter touching upon a religious community and its relationship with the national authorities.[13]

This position of the European Union is similar to that adopted by the European Court of Human Rights in the framework of the European Convention on Human Rights. The Strasbourg Court has repeatedly stated that 'where questions concerning the relationship between State and religions are at stake, on which opinion in a democratic society may reasonably differ widely, the role of the national decision-making body must be given special importance'. For the Strasbourg Court, it is not possible to discern throughout Europe a uniform conception of the significance of religion in society. Consequently, rules in this sphere will consequently vary from one country to another according to national traditions and the requirements imposed by the need to protect the rights and freedoms of others and to maintain public order. Their conclusion is that 'the choice of the extent and form such regulations should take must inevitably be left up to a point to the State concerned, as it will depend on the specific domestic context'.[14]

In other words, a broad recognition of the margin of appreciation of States does not imply a blank cheque;[15] indeed: 'This margin of appreciation goes hand in hand with a European supervision embracing both the law and the decisions applying it. The Court's task is to determine whether the measures taken at the national level were justified in principle and proportionate'.[16]

13 *Freikirche der Siebenten-Tags-Adventisten in Deutschland KdöR* (C-372/21), paragraph 24.

14 See, among many others, the case of *Leyla Şahin v. Turkey*, 10 November 2005, paragraph 109.

15 See M. Evans and P. Petkoff, 'Marginal Neutrality – Neutrality and the Margin of Appreciation in the Jurisprudence of the European Court of Human Rights', in J. Temperman, T. J. Gunn, and M. D. Evans, eds., *The European Court of Human Rights and the Freedom of Religion or Belief: The 25 Years since Kokkinakis* (Leiden/Boston: Brill Nijhoff, 2019) 128–152.

16 See the case of *Manoussakis and Others v. Greece*, 26 September 1996, paragraph 44.

III. Common Notes of the Different Models of Religion–State Relations

Three conclusions may be drawn from the above considerations: (i) there are different categories of models of state-religion relations in Europe; (ii) within each model there are differences and particularities; (iii) both the European Union and the European Court of Human Rights have competence to monitor national models and to ensure respect for EU standards and the public freedoms guaranteed by the European Convention on Human Rights.

The effectiveness of European Union law and the obligations arising from the European Convention on Human Rights for the States parties, as well as other international instruments for the protection of human rights, mean that there are elements common to the different models. These elements are present in confessional, separationist, and cooperative systems.

The first element is the protection of the fundamental right to religious freedom. This right protects all types of beliefs and convictions, provided they have a minimum of coherence, stability and seriousness, and is a precious asset not only for believers, but also for atheists, agnostics, sceptics, and the unconcerned. Moreover, this right does not refer only to *forum internum*, the protection of an area of personal autonomy and freedom, but also to *forum externum*, the right to manifest one's beliefs in public and in private and to act in accordance with them. This excludes systems of tolerance that are limited to respecting each person's beliefs in the private sphere, as all manifestations of religiosity have the right to express themselves in the public sphere.

The second element is the guarantee of equality and non-discrimination on the basis of religion. The prohibition of discrimination is a core value of EU law, to which national models of relations between the state and religions are subject,[17] and, as the European Court of Human Rights has affirmed, constitutes a 'fundamental principle' of the European Convention on Human Rights.[18]

The third element is cooperation between public authorities and religious denominations. In EU law, Article 17(3) TFEU provides that, recognising their identity and their specific contribution, the Union shall maintain an open, transparent, and regular *dialogue* with these churches and organisations. This dialogue translates into cooperation, into a

17 E. Ahlm, 'An EU Law and Religion – A Recent Development', *Canopy Forum on the Interactions of Law and Religion* (2021) 4.

18 See the cases of *S.A.S. v. France*, 1 July 2014, paragraph 149, and *Străin and Others v. Romania*, 21 July 2005, paragraph 59.

mutual understanding to channel the positive obligations incumbent on states to guarantee religious freedom and equality.[19]

Finally, the fourth element is the neutrality and impartiality of public authorities vis-à-vis religion: the European Court of Human Rights affirms that the State's duty of neutrality and impartiality is incompatible with any power on the state's part to assess the legitimacy of religious beliefs or the ways in which those beliefs are expressed.[20]

IV. The Dynamics and Evolution of Models and Their Contribution to the Maintenance of Peaceful Coexistence

The close link between the systems of relations between the state and religion and the elements that make up the identity of each nation makes it unfeasible to impose a common model to which all states must conform. On the one hand, it would not be clear what the ideal theoretical model would be that would replace the systems in force. On the other hand, such a claim would be an attack on the constitutional tradition of each state, which forms part of the foundations of the European Union. Therefore, under common elements – religious freedom, equality, cooperation, and neutrality – the systems are characterised by their diversity.

There are two dialectical relationships in the models: that between *common elements* and *diversity*, and that between *tradition* and *evolution*. Each model is defined at the highest normative level, in constitutional or foundational norms, under principles that are rooted and stable. But this does not prevent its permanent evolution in order to align itself with social changes and the progress of human rights. New legislation is introduced in response to new demands and sensitivities, and the courts develop interpretations that adapt constitutional principles to the challenges of society and to the spaces and spheres of freedom that emerge, as well as to threats to public order.

This development is not based on a unifying trend, but its paradigm is the harmonisation of models to ensure peaceful coexistence in today's secularised and multicultural societies that place great weight on individual self-determination.

In his address, Ecumenical Patriarch Bartholomew assumes the fact that the non-confessional model is prevalent in Europe and asks directly:

19 *Osmanoğlu and Kocabaş v. Switzerland*, 10 April 2017, paragraph 86.

20 *Eweida and Others v. The United Kingdom*, 15 January 2013, paragraph 81, with further references.

> is *separation* the most appropriate word for us to employ in this context?[21]

His answer is along the lines of a change of terminology from which also derives a change of approach more in line with the responsibilities of public authorities in democratic states under the rule of law:

> Instead of using what is essentially a negative word, would it not be better to speak in terms of mutual respect and cooperation?

His approach is that:

> we should not think only of separation, neutrality, or mutual tolerance but of a relationship that is far more dynamic and creative.[22]

His All-Holiness's proposal fits perfectly with the evolution of traditional models of the relationship between the state and religion. The term *toleration* evokes an era of restricted religious freedom in which the state gave preponderance to certain beliefs, while others were confined to the private sphere. The concept of *separation*, typical of the emergence of religious freedom at the end of the 18th century in France and the United States, is not appropriate in the framework of a social state obliged to adopt measures that allow the exercise of religious freedom on equal terms. Finally, the notion of *neutrality*, which is widespread in the case law of the European Court of Human Rights, is utopian and risks being interpreted as equivalent to the absence of religion from public spaces.[23] States are duty-bearers vis-à-vis their citizens and assume essential values that prevent them from being neutral. Their responsibility is to be impartial. The connotations of *impartiality* are different from those of *neutrality*. Impartiality means acting fairly and justly. To achieve this, dialogue, respect and concord are essential, as proposed by Ecumenical Patriarch Bartholomew in the address analysed here.

21 In the same vein, in Recommendation 1804 (2007) the Parliamentary Assembly of the Council of Europe pointed out: 'The Assembly reaffirms that one of Europe's shared values, transcending national differences, is the *separation of church and state*. This is a generally accepted principle that prevails in politics and institutions in democratic countries'.

22 Chryssavgis, 119.

23 M. Evans, 'State Neutrality and Religion in Europe: What's the Prospect?', 11 *Oxford Journal of Law and Religion* (2022) 4–22.

V. Conclusion

Traditional models of state-religion relations are not a valid tool for dealing with the symbiosis between secular and religious norms in the liquid and post-modern societies of the 21st century. They are only useful in describing the most characteristic features of each state in its relations with religion, but no concrete legal consequences can be drawn from them.

All these models have to accommodate the demands of religious freedom, equality, and the positive obligations of public authorities to guarantee human rights and respect for all manifestations of religiosity present in society. The aim is to combine history and tradition with secularisation, diversity and pluralism.[24]

To this end, it does not seem useful to rescue the old paradigms of separation and confine religion to the purely private sphere. Nor is it useful to proclaim specific religions as the officials of the state to the exclusion of others. The guarantee of peaceful coexistence requires cooperation with religious denominations, as this dialogue is the basis for the establishment of rules that respect religious freedom and prevent the interference of secular power in internal matters protected by the autonomy of religious groups. Ecumenical Patriarch Bartholomew's proposal on relations between the state and religions, which is based on harmonious relations that value the autonomy and dignity of each person, remains the most appropriate in present times.

24 For a developed analysis see R. McCrea, *Religion and the Public Order of the European Union* (Oxford: Oxford University Press, 2010) 16–46.

Address III

Human Rights

Orthodoxy and Human Rights
(Konrad Adenauer Foundation, Berlin, 1 June 2017)
[originally in German]

...

The attitude of the 14 Orthodox Autocephalous Churches towards human rights is not uniform. Unfortunately, there are circles and individuals in the Orthodox world who see modern human rights as a threat to our Orthodox identity. They regard human rights as a 'fundamentalism of modernity' and the conversation with and about human rights appears as an 'imported discourse'. But these people and circles do injustice to both human rights and Orthodoxy because this blocks every possibility that the Orthodox Church and theology can make a positive contribution to the topic of 'human rights'. However, that is a way to self-marginalisation ...

The attitude of the Orthodox Churches towards modernity and human rights must be based on theological criteria. Personally, we have difficulty understanding how a contemporary Orthodox theologian can think that his attitude towards modernity can only be negative.

...

On this basis, we would like to state the following on the relationship between Orthodoxy and human rights:

a) The encounter of the Orthodox Church with human rights occurs within the broader framework of its confrontation with modernity. Orthodox Christianity must finally overcome its defensive attitude towards the Enlightenment. The spirit of the Enlightenment is not in itself a threat to our identity. Like total rejection, total affirmation is not the right attitude towards modernity. A differentiated attitude is required. On the other hand, one must not confuse the true spirit of the Enlightenment with its distortions. Nor can one ignore the negative sides and impasses of modernity. ...

DOI: 10.4324/9781032636740-8

b) The demanding task of encountering Orthodox theology with modernity requires knowledge of contemporary political, social and economic realities. Without exploring modern culture, distortions are inevitable. One such distortion is the tendency to take modernity's negative dimensions to be its essence ...

c) The emphasis of the Orthodox on the social dimension of freedom, social, and community rights does not exempt us from the task of taking individual rights seriously. We insist: the protection of the individual is one thing and the individualistic narrowing of human rights is quite another. It is a misreading of the essence of human rights to characterise them as essentially individualistic. The truth is that individual rights originally refer to the social dimension of freedom. Social human rights clearly include the protection of the freedom of the individual. The dimension of fraternity or solidarity also originally belongs to human rights, something that gained new relevance in the discussion about the so-called 'third generation' of human rights.

d) Orthodoxy is often accused of ethnocentric tendencies. A more differentiated approach should be taken here, because undesirable developments in an Orthodox Church do not justify any blanket judgements about the entirety of Orthodoxy. Our thesis is that Orthodox Christianity is not ethnocentric in essence ...

It should be noted that the Orthodox Church has on many occasions denounced and condemned ethnocentrism as incompatible with the authentic traditions of Orthodoxy. When nationalism appears in an Orthodox context, it has sources other than the Orthodox faith. The encounter with modernity and human rights culture is a good opportunity for the Orthodox Church to emphasise its supranational, universal values.

e) The Orthodox Church and theology must finally accept that human rights are an achievement of modernity and that they had a secular character. This in no way means that the contribution of Christian principles and movements to their formation can be denied; because the perception of the absolute value of man is not a discovery of modernity. The commitment to respect human dignity is not a mere humane claim, it flows from the heart of the Christian gospel of love. In the context of Christianity, ethical imperatives are God's commandments, giving them emphasis and added weight.

f) We consider the idea of solidarity to be central to the encounter between Orthodoxy and human rights. On the one hand, the term solidarity refers to Christian love of one's neighbour as well as to fraternity, but at the same time it is linked to the modern history of freedom and above all to the fight for justice and equality. This makes solidarity the common point of reference for Christian social ethics and modern human rights movements.

...

As it is, our humanistic movements cannot be properly understood without reference to Christianity. We therefore consider the talk of a 'post-Christian' Europe to be inappropriate, because it ignores the fact that our present is a dimension of a Christian-inspired past that cannot easily be annulled. The expectation of a totally secularised culture has turned out to be utopian. Today we speak of 'post-secular societies'. In a totally secularised Europe, commitment to human rights would weaken.

...

In our presentation we addressed the most important challenges that the Orthodox Church is facing today. It is very important for us to emphasise that the Orthodox Church is not an escapist institution towards the coming Kingdom. She knew and she knows to give her testimony in the world courageously, which ultimately cannot be denied even by her opponents. But witnessing in the world never meant identifying with the world and its culture. When the Church's being-in-the-world is transformed into being-of-the-world, nothing positive is gained either for the Church or for the world.

...

Be that as it may, without reference to religions we can neither understand our present nor imagine our future. The fundamentalism of modernity, which sees religion as a hindrance to progress, ignores or conceals its great contribution to culture. On the other hand, it is unacceptable for religions to undermine the human rights that have made our world more humane instead of being committed to upholding them ...

We also want to mention that the lack of contours in human rights today, the expansion and stretching of their content, especially in the West, and their transformation into private claims are all tendencies that are at odds with their original political and legal objectives. They must not be used as an excuse to avoid a serious discussion with human rights and ignore their normative claims.

Certainly, in view of the human rights situation today, there is no place for triumphalism. For along with advances in human rights protection, their disregard and abuse continue. Human rights are not a secure reality today, but an ongoing task. It also remains an essential priority for our Churches, together with their commitment to the implementation of human rights, to be the place of that freedom, at the core of which is not the claiming of individual rights, but love and *diakonia*, the freedom that is not a work of man, but a gift from God.

5 Human Rights and Orthodox Christianity

Learning From Our Differences

John Witte Jr

'Ontological differences!' In 1997, that was the phrase His All-Holiness Ecumenical Patriarch Bartholomew of Constantinople used to explain the Orthodox Church's reticence about embracing the human rights reforms that Western churches were advocating for the newly liberated Soviet Union and Eastern Europe. 'The Orthodox Church is not a museum church', the Ecumenical Patriarch explained: 'It is a living church which, although keeping the old traditions from the very beginning, nevertheless understands very well the message of every new era, and it knows how to adapt itself'. The 'message' of the modern era, however, is Enlightenment liberalism, libertinism, materialism, scientism, individualism, and human rights. While Eastern Orthodoxy has resisted this modern message, Western Christianity has come under its 'shadow'. Hence the 'ontological differences' between the churches and cultures of the East and the West.

> Since the Enlightenment, the spiritual bedrock of Western civilization has been eroded and undermined. Intelligent, well-intentioned people sincerely believed that the wonders of science could replace the miracles of faith. But these great minds missed one vital truth – that faith is not a garment to be slipped on and off; it is a quality of the human spirit, from which it is inseparable.

'There are a few things [the West] can learn from the Orthodox Church', His All-Holiness declared – not least 'that, paradoxically, faith can endure without freedom, but freedom cannot long abide without faith'.[1]

Twenty years later, in his 2017 Berlin Lecture on 'Orthodoxy and Human Rights', Ecumenical Patriarch Bartholomew echoed and elaborated some of these same themes. He continued to argue that human

1 'Address of His All-Holiness Ecumenical Patriarch Bartholomew Phos Hilaron, "Joyful Light"', Georgetown University, Washington, DC, 21 October 1997, quoted in *Washington Post* (25 October 1997), H12.

DOI: 10.4324/9781032636740-9

rights were shaped by the 18th-century Enlightenment, with its false 'optimistic anthropology', 'its forgetfulness of sins, its rationalism, individualism and autonomism'. He repeated common Orthodox worries that the 1948 Universal Declaration of Human Rights was a 'smug' 'humanistic manifesto' and a secular 'Trojan horse' filled with dangerous modernist ideas that threatened the heart and soul of Orthodox faith, family, morality, and nationhood. And he repeated recent warnings that the newly liberated Orthodox Churches of the Soviet bloc and Eastern Europe were being forced to compete with Western missionising faiths in an open marketplace of religious ideas, without having the experiences or resources needed to compete.[2]

In this same 2017 lecture, however, the Patriarch also pushed beyond these 'ontological differences'. He now stated that human rights ideals of liberty, equality, dignity, and fraternity had been 'rooted in Christian culture' before the Enlightenment and could still be 'nourished from that deep Christian freedom, freedom through faith, expressed in selfless love'. He stressed that faith and freedom together could 'mobilize forces of solidarity in man and spur him on the fight against justice and for a more humane world'. He urged all Christians to embrace 'solidarity, peace and reconciliation and … protection of fundamental human rights'. He encouraged his fellow Orthodox Christians not to reject modernity altogether, but to embrace its promise of individual freedom while also demonstrating the 'power of social freedom'. He further encouraged the Orthodox faithful not to equate modernity with secularism alone, but to appreciate the diverse 'political, social, and economic realities' of the modern world. And he encouraged the Orthodox faithful to look beyond the separatism, secularism, and *laïcité* of some Western laws and appreciate that some modern Western nations still established Christianity and shared the Orthodox appreciation for 'the close relationship between church, people, and state'. 'Human rights will remain a major concern for mankind in the future', the Patriarch concluded, and it is an

> essential priority for our churches, together with their commitment to the implementation of human rights, to be the place of that freedom at the core of which is not the claiming of individual rights, but love and the *diakonia*, the freedom that is not a work of man but a gift from God.[3]

2 'For Human Rights: HAH Lecture at the Headquarters of the Konrad Adenauer Foundation in Berlin' (1 June 2017).

3 Ibid. See further discussion in A.G. Roeber, *Orthodox Christians and the Rights Revolution in America* (New York: Fordham University Press, 2023).

Ecumenical Patriarch Bartholomew's growing appreciation for the mutually beneficial interaction of Christianity and human rights offers new hope for deeper Christian ecumenism and broader religious collaboration in support of human rights around the world. The 'ontological differences' between Western and Eastern Christians remain real and require continued conversation to foster better mutual understanding. The next two sections of this chapter take up two areas of difference today, but the chapter concludes with a couple of illustrations of what Western churches and human rights advocates 'can learn from the Orthodox Church', as Patriarch Bartholomew put it.

I. Baptism, Mission, and Conversion

Ironically, it was the liberation of traditional Orthodox lands in the 1990s that highlighted one area of intense 'ontological difference' today – that between Eastern and Western Christian views of baptism, mission, and conversion. Mikhail Gorbachev's campaigns of *glasnost* and *perestroika* in the late 1980s soon led to the implosion of the Soviet Union and eventual dissolution of Soviet bloc lands from the Baltics to the Balkans. Russia and several Eastern European countries threw off their Communist yokes and created new Western-style constitutions and ratified many of the most progressive international human rights instruments.[4]

This rapid political transformation not only liberated local Orthodox and other churches, but also opened these societies to foreign religious groups, who were granted rights to enter these regions for the first time in decades. After 1990, these foreign missionaries came in increasing numbers to preach their faiths, to offer their services, to share their literature, to build new schools, to establish new charities, and to convert new souls. Initially, Orthodox and local religious groups welcomed these foreigners, particularly their co-religionists abroad with whom they had lost real contact for many decades.

But within a decade local Orthodox leaders came to resent these foreign missionaries, particularly those from North America, Western Europe, South Korea, and elsewhere who assumed a democratic human rights ethic. Local religious groups resented the participation in the marketplace of religious ideas that democracy assumes. They resented the toxic waves of materialism and individualism that democracy inflicts. They resented the massive expansion of religious pluralism that democracy

4 M. Bourdeaux, *Gorbachev, Glasnost, and Gospel* (London: Hodder & Stoughton, 1990); J. Witte, Jr. and M. Bourdeaux, eds., *Proselytism and Orthodoxy in Russia: The New War for Souls* (Maryknoll, NY: Orbis Books, 1999); P. Valliere and R. Poole, eds., *Law and the Christian Tradition in Modern Russia* (London: Routledge, 2022).

encourages. They resented the extravagant forms of religious speech, press, and assembly that democracy protects.[5]

A new war for souls thus broke out in these regions – a war to reclaim the traditional Orthodox souls of these newly opened societies and a war to retain adherence and adherents to the Orthodox Church. In part, this was a legal war – as local Orthodox leaders pressured their political leaders to adopt statutes and regulations restricting the constitutional rights of their foreign religious rivals. Beneath shiny constitutional veneers of religious freedom for all and unqualified ratification of international human rights instruments, several Orthodox majority countries in the 1990s and early 2000s passed firm new anti-proselytism laws, cult registration requirements, tightened visa controls, and various discriminatory restrictions on new or newly arrived religions. Those policies have continued in some Eastern European lands today, driving beleaguered religious minorities and foreigners to seek protection from the European Court of Human Rights.[6]

In part, this was a theological war between fundamentally different theologies about the nature and purpose of mission. Western Christians, particularly Evangelicals, assume that in order to be saved every person must make a personal, conscious commitment to Christ – to be born again, to convert. Any person who has not been born again, or who once reborn now leads a nominal or non-Christian life, is a legitimate object of evangelism – regardless of whether and where the person has already been baptised. The principal means of reaching that person is through proclamation and demonstration of the Gospel. Any region that has not been open to the Gospel is a legitimate 'foreign mission field' – regardless of whether the region might have another majority Christian church in place. Under this definition of mission, traditional Orthodox lands, where the Communist yoke had long suppressed the Gospel, are prime targets for Christian witness.[7]

The Orthodox Church, too, believes that each person must come into a personal relationship with Christ in order to be saved. But such a relationship comes more through birth than rebirth, and more through regular sacramental living than a one-time conversion. A person who is born into the Orthodox Church has by definition started '*theosis*' – the process of becoming 'acceptable to God' and ultimately 'coming into eternal

5 Symposium, 'Soul Wars in Russia', 12 *Emory International Law Review* (1998): 1–738; Symposium, 'Pluralism, Proselytism and Nationalism in Eastern Europe', 36 *Journal of Ecumenical Studies* (1999) 1–286.

6 See cases in J. Witte, Jr. and A. Pin, 'Faith in Strasbourg and Luxembourg: The Fresh Rise of Religious Freedom Litigation in the Pan-European Courts', 70 *Emory Law Journal* (2021) 587–661.

7 *Proselytism and Orthodoxy*, 108–226.

communion with Him'. Through infant baptism, and later through the mass, the Eucharist, the icons, and other services of the church, a person slowly comes into fuller realisation of this divine communion.[8] Proclamation of the Gospel is certainly a legitimate means of aiding the process of *theosis* – and is especially effective in reaching those not born into the Orthodox Church. But, for the Orthodox, 'mission does not aim primarily at the transmission of moral and intellectual convictions and truths, but at the ... incorporation of persons into the communion that exists in God and in the Church'.[9]

This theology has led the Orthodox Church to a quite different understanding of the proper venue and object of evangelism. Traditional Orthodox lands are hardly an open 'mission field' which other Christians are free to harvest. On the contrary, this territory and population are under the 'spiritual protectorate' of the Orthodox Church. Any person who has been baptised into the Orthodox Church is no longer a legitimate object of evangelism – regardless of whether that person leads only a nominal or non-Christian life. Only if that person actively spurns the Orthodox Church are they open to the evangelism of others.

This is the theological source of the Orthodox clergy's complaints about the proselytising activity of many Western churches in their traditional homelands. They are not only complaining about improper methods of evangelism – bribery, blackmail, coercion, and material inducements used by some groups; the garish carnivals, flashy billboards, and expensive media blitzes used by other faiths. They are also complaining about the improper presence of missionaries – those who have come not to aid the Orthodox Church in its mission, but to compete with the Orthodox Church for its own souls on its own territory.[10]

Human rights norms alone will ultimately do little to resolve this fundamental theological difference between Orthodox and Western Christians. 'In seeking to limit the incursion of missionary activity we often are accused of violating the right to freedom of conscience and the restriction of individual rights', Russian Orthodox Patriarch Aleksii II explained in 1997 during the height of the soul wars in Russia.

> But freedom does not mean general license. The truth of Christ which sets us free (John 8:32) also places upon us a great responsibility, to

8 Ibid., 31–77.

9 J. A. Nichols, 'Mission, Evangelism, and Proselytism in Christianity: Mainline Conceptions as Reflected in Church Documents', 12 *Emory International Law Review* (1999) 563–650, at 624.

10 See H. J. Berman, 'Freedom of Religion in Russia: An Amicus Brief for the Defendant', in *Proselytism and Orthodoxy*, 261–283.

> respect and preserve the freedom of others. However, the aggressive imposition by foreign missionaries of views and principles which come from a religious and cultural environment which is strange to us, is in fact a violation of both [our] religious and civil rights.[11]

The Orthodox Church must be as free in the exercise of its missiology as Western Evangelicals wish to be. Both groups' rights, when fully exercised, will inevitably clash.

The 30-year war for souls in traditional Orthodox lands requires a theological resolution as much as a human rights resolution. Interreligious dialogue, education, and cooperation sound like tried and tired remedies, but these are essential first steps. Self-imposed guidelines of prudential mission work by Western Christians are essential steps as well: know and appreciate Orthodox history, culture, and language; avoid Westernisation of the Gospel and First Amendmentisation of politics; deal honestly and respectfully with theological and liturgical differences; respect and advocate the religious rights of all peoples; be Good Samaritans before good preachers; proclaim the Gospel in word and deed.[12] Such steps will slowly bring current antagonists beyond caricatures into a greater mutual understanding, and a greater unity in diversity.

The ultimate theological guide to resolving the deeper conflict over mission and conversion, however, must be a more careful balancing of the Great Commission and the Golden Rule. Christ called his followers to mission: 'Go therefore and make disciples of all nations …' (Matt. 28:19). But Christ also called his followers to exercise restraint and respect: 'Do unto others, as you would have done unto you' (Matt. 7:12). If both sides in the current war for souls would strive to hold these principles in better balance, their dogmatism might be tempered and their conflicts assuaged.

II. Church, State, Nation

A related ontological difference between Eastern and Western Christianity is reflected in the Orthodox Church's attitude toward the state. The Orthodox Church has no concept akin to the Western dualistic constructions of two cities, two powers, two swords, two kingdoms, two realms – let alone a 'high and impregnable wall of separation between church and state'.[13] The Orthodox world, rooted in the ancient Byzantine Empire,

11 Quoted in *Proselytism and Orthodoxy*, 22–23.

12 See examples in ibid., 185–196, 323–340.

13 See J. Witte, Jr., 'Facts and Fictions About the History of Separation of Church and State', 48 *Journal of Church and State* (2006) 15–46.

views church and state as an organic community, united by blood and soil, a veritable symphonia of religion, politics, society, language, ethnicity, and national culture.[14]

For many centuries, this organic unity of church, state, and nation gave the Orthodox clergy a unique spiritual and moral voice in traditional Orthodox societies, and unique access to the power, privilege, and protection of the political authorities. It allowed the Orthodox clergy to lead and comfort Orthodox lands in times of great crisis – during the Hun, Mongol, Magyar, and Ottoman invasions, the Napoleonic Wars, the Turkish genocide, the great World Wars, and more. It allowed the Orthodox Church to heal and teach these societies through its schools and monasteries, its literature and preaching. It also allowed the Orthodox clergy to nourish and inspire the people through the power and pathos of its liturgy, icons, prayers, and music.

But this organic unity also subjected the Orthodox Churches to substantial state control over their polities and properties, and substantial restrictions on its religious ministry and prophecy. It also required them to be obedient and supportive of the political authorities. In return for their subservience, the Orthodox clergy could turn to the state to protect them against religious outsiders and competition. A poignant illustration of this is offered by Joachim, the Patriarch of Moscow at the turn of the 18th century. In a 1690 testament, the Patriarch implored co-Tsars Ivan and Peter 'never to allow any Orthodox Christians in their realm to entertain any close friendly relations with heretics and dissenters – with Latins, Lutherans, Calvinists, and Tatars'. He further urged the tsars to pass a decree 'that men of foreign creeds who come here to this pious realm shall under no circumstances preach their religion, disparage our faith in any conversations or introduce their alien customs derived from their heresies for the temptation of Christians'. 'Such was the position of the Muscovite Church', leading Russian historian Firuz Kazemzadeh concludes, 'and such, in essence, it has remained' not only in Russia but in many parts of the Orthodox world today.[15]

We can easily read the recent Orthodox Church–state alliances in fighting against foreign missionaries and faiths as yet another act in this centuries-long drama. And, in turn, we can see the sad condonation of the current Moscow Patriarchate in Russia's outrageous war in Ukraine as

14 See J. McGuckin, *The Ascent of Christian Law: Patristic and Byzantine Formulations of a New Civilization* (Yonkers, NY: St. Vladimir's Seminary Press, 2012).

15 F. Kazemzadeh, 'Reflections on Church and State in Russian History' in *Proselytism and Orthodoxy*, 227–238, at 236; see further R.P. Geraci and M. Khodarkovsky, eds., *Of Religion and Empire: Missions, Conversion, and Tolerance in Tsarist Russia* (Ithaca, NY: Cornell University Press, 2001).

the necessary price for the Orthodox Church to pay for Putin's ongoing protection and patronage.

With this 'ontological difference', too, simple invocations of religious freedom norms, American-style separatism, or French-style *laïcité*, will do little to assuage these conflicts between East and West. Western Christians must appreciate that their own long history of church–state relations featured a variety of constitutional forms and norms, some of them rather close to the symphonia of Orthodox lands. They must also remember the adage of Oliver Wendell Holmes, Jr that '[t]he life of the law is not logic but experience'.[16] Constitutional laws are not commodities to be imported or exported en masse to other nations. These laws must grow out of the souls and soils of the people who create and live under them, who breathe into them their own cultures and experiences, their own *Volksgeist* as Otto von Gierke put it. Western formulations of human rights, religious freedom, and church–state relations cannot and should not be fully duplicated or imitated in Orthodox lands. Indeed, the sobering lesson learned during the heady days of glasnost and perestroika was that the full-scale importation of these Western constitutional norms created a toxic compound that these long-closed societies had little capacity to absorb. The better course for Orthodox lands is to use Western constitutional and human rights norms as a valuable resource and inspiration for gradually reconstructing a better constitutional order for the protection of individual and institutional religious freedom for all their people.

Orthodox Christians, in turn, must appreciate that modern norms of human rights and religious freedom are not creations of the Western Enlightenment nor a ward under the exclusive patronage of its secular liberal values. A veritable cottage industry of recent new scholarship has documented the long history of rights talk before the Enlightenment. We now know a great deal more about classical Roman understandings of rights (*iura*), liberties (*libertates*), capacities (*facultates*), powers (*potestates*), and related concepts, and their elaboration by medieval and early modern civilians. We can now pore over an intricate latticework of arguments about individual and group rights and liberties developed by medieval Catholic canonists and moralists. We can now trace the ample expansion and reform of this medieval handiwork by neo-scholastic writers in early modern Spain and Portugal and by Lutheran, Anglican, and Calvinist Protestants on the Continent and in Great Britain and their colonies. We now know a good deal more about classical republican theories of liberty developed in Greece and Rome, and their transformative influence on early modern common lawyers and political revolutionaries on both sides

16 O.W. Holmes, Jr., *The Common Law* (Boston: Little, Brown, 1881) 1.

of the Atlantic. We now know, in brief, that the West knew ample 'liberty before liberalism'[17] and had many fundamental rights in place before there were modern democratic revolutions fought in their name. It is a telling anecdote that by 1650 almost every right listed 150 years later in the French Declaration of the Rights of Man and Citizen (1789) and the United States Bill of Rights (1791) had already been defined, defended, and died for by Christians on both sides of the Atlantic.[18]

To be sure, some modern human rights advocates have deprecated and sometimes denied these Christian roots, and many current formulations of human rights are suffused with fundamental liberal beliefs and values, some of which run counter to cardinal Christian beliefs. But liberalism does not and should not have a monopoly on the nurture of human rights. The law of human rights norms is the *ius gentium* of our times, the common law of nations, which ultimately depends on a variety of beliefs and values, institutions and communities that will constantly shape and reshape it, that will constantly challenge it to improve.

III. What Orthodoxy Can Teach Us about Human Rights

Among these communities, the Eastern Orthodox have immense spiritual resources, whose implications for human rights are only now beginning to be seen. These spiritual resources lie, in part, in Orthodox worship – the passion of the liturgy, the pathos of the icons, and the power of spiritual silence. They lie, in part, in Orthodox Church life – the distinct balancing between hierarchy and congregationalism through autocephaly; between uniform worship and liturgical freedom through alternative vernacular rites; between community and individuality through a trinitarian communalism, which is centred on the parish, on the extended family, on the wizened grandmother (the 'babushka' in Russia). These spiritual resources lie, in part, in the massive martyrdom of millions of Orthodox faithful in the 20th century – whether suffered by Russian Orthodox under the Communist Party, by Greek and Armenian Orthodox under Turkish and Iranian radicals, by Middle Eastern Copts at the hands of religious extremists, or by North African Orthodox under all manner of fascist autocrats and tribal strongmen.[19]

17 Q. Skinner, *Liberty Before Liberalism* (Cambridge: Cambridge University Press, 2012).

18 See J. Witte, Jr, *The Blessings of Liberty: Human Rights and Religious Freedom in the Western Legal Tradition* (Cambridge: Cambridge University Press, 2021).

19 J. H. Billington, 'Orthodox Christianity and the Russian Transformation', in *Proselytism and Orthodoxy*, 51–65.

These deep spiritual resources of the Orthodox Church have no exact parallels in modern Catholicism and Protestantism, and most of their implications for law, politics, and society have still to be drawn out. It would be wise to hear what an ancient church, newly charred and chastened by decades of oppression and martyrdom, considers essential to the regime of religious freedom. It would be enlightening to watch how ancient Orthodox communities, still largely centred on the parish and the family, will reconstruct social and economic order and attendant rights. It would be prudent to see how a culture, more prone to beautifying than to analysing, might transform our understanding of culture. It would be instructive to listen to how a tradition that still celebrates spiritual silence as its highest virtue might recast the meaning of freedom of speech and expression. It would be illuminating to feel how a people who have long cherished and celebrated the role of the woman – the wizened babushka of the home, the faithful remnant in the parish pews, the living icon of the Assumption of the Mother of God – might elaborate the place of women and the meaning of women's rights in church, state, and society.[20]

IV. Conclusion

Ecumenical Patriarch Bartholomew was certainly wise to remind us that '[t]here are a few things' that Western churches and states 'can learn from the Orthodox Church'. We would do well to listen and learn as Orthodox Churches embrace more fully the global ecumenical project, and as Orthodox majority lands come into greater contact with the rest of the world. Particularly on questions of law, religion, and human rights, the world needs new wise men from the East.

20 Ibid.; see also A. Papanikolau, *The Mystical as Political: Democracy and Non-Radical Orthodoxy* (Notre Dame, IN: University of Notre Dame Press, 2012).

6 Better Human Rights

The Orthodox Lesson

Andrea Pin

With his address *Orthodoxy and Human Rights*, Ecumenical Patriarch Bartholomew has taken an extremely honest look at the relationship of Orthodox Christianity to human rights. He is historically honest, as he acknowledges the many centuries of tensions and conflicts that have characterised this relationship. He is pragmatically honest, as he admits that such tensions still exist and will not fade away anytime soon, and that, therefore, religious narratives and human rights narratives should look for common ground and mutual understanding. He is epistemologically honest, as he addresses the anthropological and theological roots of such tensions, suggesting that reconciliations will inevitably be partial and dynamic.

His All-Holiness' speech, however, is also optimistic. He looks forward to discovering how these twin forces will play out and shape our postmodern world. In his words, the 'tension' between them 'can be beneficial for a fruitful dialogue'. His honesty, realism, and optimism about the future of dialogue between Christianity and human rights make his address compelling.

I. Beyond Conflicts Between Religion and Human Rights

His All-Holiness argues that born as a 'dynamic reality that was able to respond to the great challenges associated with the living conditions of modernity' and 'as a valuable instrument of humanism in politics and law', human rights have 'faced opposition from the Christian Churches' since the first emergence of human rights. Churches resisted the language and logic of rights, he states, until they saw 'the catastrophic consequences and the indescribable inhumanity of the twentieth century', which 'made the humane goal of human rights [the churches'] own concern'. The churches' resistance arose, he states, because '[h]uman rights do not belong to the traditional good of religions'.

Such statements are probably grimmer than reality. Some legal historians would actually argue that there is a deep historical connection and

DOI: 10.4324/9781032636740-10

continuity between Christianity and rights that goes back several centuries. But this chapter is not the place for such an analysis; and I happily defer this task to those better equipped to undertake it. Instead, I focus on how and why the Ecumenical Patriarch sees a potential in the interplay between religion and human rights by pointing to the notion of 'dignity'. He believes that the idea of dignity can unlock such a potential, as it constitutes 'the normative basis of human rights' and 'includes the equality of all human beings and the inalienability of fundamental human rights'. In his words, 'the common concern for human dignity – despite the differences in the foundation of this dignity – actually connects religions and human rights movements with each other'.

This chapter reflects on the Ecumenical Patriarch's emphasis on dignity; then it sheds light on his view of the conflict between Christianity and human rights; finally, it considers his encouragement that human rights advocates adopt a broader understanding of the human person and that the Orthodox Church embraces rights as an asset for the postmodern world. What follows partly confirms the Ecumenical Patriarch's diagnosis, and partially challenges it by arguing that the connection between Christianity and human rights through the prism of dignity is much stronger and deeper than what he seems to believe.

His All-Holiness' bet on dignity is well-founded. The Universal Declaration of Human Rights, the document that spurred a global interest in the notion of dignity by encouraging its incorporation into constitutional texts and case law, had dignity as its 'basic woof'.[1] However, dignity has gained a prominent role in contemporary legal thought due to contributions of both religious and secular voices. Neither supporters of human rights nor advocates of the political role of Christianity and religion more broadly can claim any monopoly over the concept of dignity.

II. Human Nature and Human Rights: The Place of Dignity

Dignity has a hybrid lineage. Religious thought and secular thought have converged in shaping the notion for centuries, although many believe that religion and human rights long kept each other at bay before meeting only in late modernity and simply for practical purposes.

Scholars such as Catherine Dupré have isolated the founding moments of the secular idea of dignity, arguing that the notion developed along a-religious or even anti-religious lines. Dupré found the first moment

1 T. Lindholm, 'Article 1', in Asbjørn Eide et al. eds., *The Universal Declaration of Human Rights: A Commentary* (Oslo: Scandinavian University Press, 1992) 34.

in the works of the Renaissance's intellectual titan Pico della Mirandola, who identified the very nature of human beings as their capacity to rise above their instinctual needs and give shape to their own fate through the exercise of their freedom.[2] She found the second moment in the rise of the egalitarian, libertarian, and solidaristic spirit of the French Revolution. The revolutionary values dismantled the hierarchical social structure of the *Ancien Régime* and implemented a new political order that was based on equal rights and mutual duties of brotherhood.[3] The third founding moment was Kant's conceptualisation that human beings should always be treated as ends in themselves, and never as means.[4] In Dupré's narrative, these historical turns broke the cultural monopoly of ancient authoritarian, unequal, God-centred, ontological understandings of dignity. The 1848 French legislation that outlawed slavery was the first legal appearance of this conceptualisation of human dignity in a document of constitutional salience.[5] From then on, the same understanding would sporadically appear in constitutional texts before being crystallised in the Universal Declaration of Human Rights.

Seeing the success of dignity as a legal and constitutional trajectory born out of secularisation and the repudiation of Christianity in the West requires selective reading. It handpicks strands of legal thinking that resonate with this theory while disregarding other significant factors that helped shape the concept. The theoretical and legal developments that made the idea of human dignity shine in the 20th century were not just the offspring of secular thinking.

The genealogy of dignity centred on secular narratives overlooks the centuries-long efforts of Catholic theologians and philosophers who advocated in favour of indigenous peoples and against slavery in Latin America. These Christian intellectuals helped to shape the notion that all human beings are endowed with certain inalienable rights and are worthy of respect regardless of their personal or social conditions:[6] an emphasis that Simon Bolivar later retrieved to claim freedom for the oppressed peoples of Latin America.[7]

The Christian contribution to the development of human dignity as a key legal notion was not episodical. French Catholic environments between the late 19th century and the 1930s helped to sharpen the

2 C. Dupré, *The Age of Dignity: Human Rights and Constitutionalism in Europe* (Oxford and Portland, Or.: Hart Publishing, 2015) 32.

3 Ibid., 39 and 43.

4 Ibid., 39 and 43.

5 Ibid., 50.

6 See P.G. Carozza, 'From Conquest to Constitutions: Retrieving a Latin American Tradition of the Idea of Human Rights', 25 *Human Rights Quarterly* (2003) 281–313, 292–295.

7 Ibid., 301, n. 102.

concept further, when philosophical personalism and social Catholicism pushed for a bold affirmation of the value of the person through the prism of dignity,[8] with ramifications across the Old as well as the New World.[9] After the turn of the century, the 1919 Weimar constitutional reference to 'human dignity' in the field of social rights also emerged as a product of Christian cultural strands.[10]

The notion of dignity as a powerful legal concept went beyond intellectual circles and found support also among the leaders of Christianity. The late 19th-century encyclicals of Leo XIII and documents released under Pius XI and Pius XII in the 1930s and 1940s echoed these intellectual developments and progressively expounded this understanding of dignity.[11] Pius XI used this concept in two encyclicals: *Mit brennender Sorge* (14 March 1937) against Nazism and *Divini Redemptoris* (19 March 1937) against communism. The Catholic Church later repeatedly used this idea of human dignity: '[t]hanks to Pius XII, in fact, individual dignity became an incredibly common concept across the Atlantic during the later phases' of World War II.[12]

However, the most telling example of Christian influence on the legal success of dignity is the 1937 Irish Constitution. Promulgated shortly after the two pontifical documents, it was deeply influenced by Catholic teaching. The main drafter of the Constitution, the political leader Eamon de Valera, was familiar with the neo-Scholastic circles that promoted the idea of human dignity and shared critical points in the text, including the mention of dignity, with the papal nuncio in Ireland.[13]

Contrary to what His All-Holiness seems to believe, key concepts of contemporary human rights discourse, such as human dignity, did not develop in tension with religion and Christianity. Actually, Christianity was one of the driving forces that shaped and spread it. There is no need to bring human rights and religion close – they have hardly kept apart in this matter. Paradoxically, this short perusal of the religious sources of dignity confirms the optimism of the Ecumenical Patriarch for the possibility of reconciling human rights and Christianity. If a notion such as

8 S. Moyn, 'The Secret History of Human Dignity', in C. McCrudden, ed., *Understanding Human Dignity* (Oxford: Oxford University Press, 2013) 99.

9 Ibid.

10 J. Luther, 'Ragionevolezza e dignità umana' 5 (Dipartimento di Politiche pubbliche e scelte collettive – POLIS Working Paper No. 79/2006), http://polis.unipmn.it/pubbl/RePEc/uca/ucapdv/luther79.pdf [https://perma.cc/4C5X-CFM5].

11 G.J. Staab, *The Dignity of Man in Modern Papal Doctrine: Leo XIII to Pius XII* (Washington, D.C.: The Catholic University of America, 1957) 11.

12 C. Goos, 'Wurde des Menschen: Restoring Human Dignity in Post-Nazi Germany', in McCrudden, ed., *Understanding Human Dignity*, op cit., 92.

13 Moyn, op cit., 54.

dignity arose as a result of collaboration among different worldviews, we can be reasonably confident that similar collaborations may materialise again.

For a new era of mutual collaborations to begin, however, His All-Holiness emphasises that 'much depends on the attitude of religions towards [human rights]'. In his diagnosis, religions are all but passive players. They cannot simply expect human rights to become something else – they need to participate actively in their development and also seize the opportunities to understand human rights in religious terms.

His All-Holiness' diagnosis of the tensions between contemporary religious and secular understandings of dignity, however, is hardly disputable. Multiple conflicts have arisen lately, and the Ecumenical Patriarch correctly identifies some key aspects that have made the confrontations so fundamental and sometimes even harsh.

III. Why Christianity and Human Rights Collide, and Why They Should Not

Frictions between human rights and religion is not a monopoly of Christianity. As Ecumenical Patriarch Bartholomew correctly points out, non-Christian groups have constantly – and perhaps increasingly – criticised human rights as the offspring of colonial, Western-centred cultural hegemony. They would be either plagued with secularism and individualism or saturated with Christian values.

However, Orthodox Christianity, His All-Holiness argues, has a specific anthropology that makes the relationship with human rights even more fraught. The Orthodox understanding of human beings especially clashes with some conceptualisations of human rights that, in his view, are too narrow or simplistic. The 'Orthodox ideal in respect of human dignity', he observes, does not downplay the role of rights; on the contrary. In fact, 'the believer has an additional motivation to stand up for the rights of fellow human beings'. The Christian faith, however, 'transcends the horizon of established human rights'. For 'Orthodox theology, the "highest ethos" is self-sacrificing love, i.e. the voluntary renunciation of one's own individual rights in the name of one's neighbour'.

The self-sacrificing value of Christian love, Bartholomew continues, resonates with the strong belief in the 'social content of freedom'. This is not merely a theoretical notion, His All-Holiness remarks, as it is empirically visible in the 'radical communal orientation of some cultures'. This is the case of Orthodox Christianity, for which 'being a person always means being with, being in community with other people'. Overlooking this component of human personhood 'undermines the foundations of social values, of family, of religion and nation and threatens fundamental moral values', as the Patriarch emphasises, drawing from the Holy and Great Council of the Orthodox.

His All-Holiness' accusation that a too narrow reading of humanity leaves out too much of our individual and social life resonates with the view of some contemporary legal thinkers with a strong religious background, such as the Jewish scholar Joseph Weiler. When considering post-World War II Europe, Weiler notes that the complex judicial infrastructure that connects the national and the supranational levels of the government has created a rich network of courts that has unavoidably focused on the claims of the individual in a cultural process that, 'little by little, almost without realizing it', has turned the average European citizen 'into a self-centred individual' apart from the broader community she lives within.[14] In other words, this emphasis on the rights of the individual overlooks what individuals owe to each other and to broader society. The Anglican priest and scholar Nigel Biggar has also fiercely denounced this phenomenon, noting that within judicial activity are visible 'signs of a rights-fundamentalism and a deficiency in historical imagination'.[15] It is not so surprising, then, that parts of the Christian sphere have given their support to leaders who claim to represent 'illiberal' constitutionalism and emphasise collective needs as an antidote to the excesses of rights-based narratives.[16]

While His All-Holiness criticises the shortcomings of a culture of rights that runs the risk of being self-centred, and that thus encourages modernity to take a fresh look at the relational component of humanity, he also acknowledges the efforts that Orthodoxy must exert to understand modernity. Instead of being content with criticising the modern and postmodern culture of rights, he asks himself and his church what is the right thing for them to do, given the current circumstances.

Bartholomew first insists that Orthodox anthropology and modern human rights anthropology may not be the same, but they are not necessarily bound to clash with each other. A dialogue between them is possible. But to rise in such a new era, Orthodoxy must understand the 'contemporary political, social and economic realities. Without exploring modern culture, distortions are inevitable'.

14 J.H.H. Weiler, 'Covid, Europe, and Democratic Self-Asphyxiation', in M. Poiares Maduro and P.W. Kahn, eds., *Democracy in Times of Pandemic* (Cambridge: Cambridge University Press, 2020) 150.

15 N. Biggar, *What Is Wrong with Rights?* (Oxford: Oxford University Press, 2020) 309.

16 A. Pin and L.P. Vanoni, 'Catholicism, Liberalism, and Populism', 46 *Brigham Young University Law Review* (2021) 1301–1328, 1312.

The step he proposes is all but obvious. Contemporary critics of human rights[17] often put modernity on trial for misunderstanding human nature; here, the Ecumenical Patriarch argues that Christianity can also misunderstand modernity. Superficiality is a risk for everyone, not just for the secular, modern, and postmodern world.

Bartholomew then experiments with his own proposal that Christianity look to itself and reconsider its strategies. He openly acknowledges that emphasising the 'social dimension of freedom, social and community rights does not exempt us from the task of taking individual rights seriously'. Or, in other words, '[i]t is a misreading of the essence of human rights to characterize them as essentially individualistic'. The 'lack of contours in human rights today, the expansion and stretching of their content ... and their transformation into private claims' cannot 'be used as an excuse to avoid a serious discussion with human rights and ignore their normative claims'. Orthodoxy must avoid caricaturing individual rights as merely individualistic or hedonistic.

Bartholomew doubles down and explains that Orthodox Christianity needs to purify and propose itself to the contemporary world in a fruitful way. He specifically addresses the charges that Orthodoxy has embraced a nationalist, chauvinist, identity-focused political agenda. He seems to say that the Orthodox Church must respect the line that separates the 'particularly close relationship between Church, people and state' that Orthodoxy displayed when its churches participated 'in the liberation struggles of the Orthodox peoples' from 'nationalism', which appears in an Orthodox context but 'has sources other than the orthodox faith'.

This statement by the Ecumenical Patriarch of Orthodoxy is particularly significant. In the 1990s, after the collapse of communist regimes, Christianity was often deployed to reinforce the sense of national sovereignty and pride among countries that had freed themselves from Soviet dominance. Sometimes this process strengthened the connection between state authority and religious authority, constraining the religious freedom of religious minorities and Orthodox majorities alike. Eastern European states have thus made repeated attempts to preserve the unity of the Orthodox Church within their territories and to oversee its internal affairs, attracting criticism from the European Court of Human Rights more than once.[18] Therefore, the Ecumenical Patriarch's words distance him and the Orthodox Church more broadly from extreme forms of equating religious and national identity that discriminate against religious

17 On the critics of human rights, see J. Witte, Jr, *The Blessings of Liberty* (Cambridge: Cambridge University Press, 2021) 15.

18 For example, see *Serif v. Greece*, App. no. 38178/97; *Metropolitan Church of Bessarabia v. Moldova*, App. no. 45701/99; *Holy Synod of the Bulgarian Orthodox Church et al v. Bulgaria*, App. nn. 412/03 and 35677/04; *Svyato-Mykhaylivska Parafiya v. Ukraine*, App. no. 77703/01.

minorities and dissidents, and he warns against making religion a branch of government.

IV. The Role of Christianity in Human Rights Discourse

His All-Holiness does not just recommend that Orthodoxy take a fresh look at the role and meaning of human rights. One of the most compelling and provocative parts of his address is the broader strategy he lays out for the Orthodox Church in contemporary societies.

His address is not an endorsement of contemporary narratives about human beings, society, and politics. The most evident line of criticism is probably the statement that '[t]he European idea cannot be limited to economic objectives or other pragmatic-technocratic orientations. It also has a spiritual, humanistic and cultural aspect'. This is where Christianity can play a role: to recover an outward, social, non-self-referential approach, contemporary Europe needs to retrieve its transcendent soul.

The Ecumenical Patriarch's call for a transcendent perspective on politics, law, and human rights is not obvious. Professor András Sajó, a former judge of the European Court of Human Rights, once wrote – in defence of a non-transcendent political perspective – that 'Constitutionalism exists only where the society does not take into public consideration transcendental concerns'.[19] Bartholomew, however, has good theoretical and legal allies on his side. On the religious plane, the late Benedict XVI spoke time and again about the necessity of understanding the legal realm as open to transcendence. In a series of famous speeches, Benedict argued that polities cannot understand themselves as self-referential universes; they should instead admit that their members belong also to an order that exceeds them.[20]

This call for transcendence is not limited to religious leaders and intellectuals who argue for a bigger role for themselves and their communities. The notion of dignity and the entire edifice of human rights that was born out of the ashes of World War II responded to the need for legal orders to understand their limits and make room for what exceeds them. Looking at the processes of nation and constitution building of the early 1950s, the Lebanese philosopher Charles Malik, one of the greatest drafters, defenders, and theorists of the Universal Declaration of Human Rights, asked himself: 'What is the ultimate trouble with the

19 A. Sajó, 'Preliminaries to a Concept of Constitutional Secularism', *International Journal of Constitutional Law* (2008) 605–629, 618.

20 A. Pin, 'A Listening Heart: Where Democracy Begins', in M. Cartabia and A. Simoncini, eds., *Pope Benedict XVI's Legal Thought* ((New York: Cambridge University Press, 2015) 215–216.

world today?' His own reply to the question was, 'It is the loss of the dimension of transcendence'.[21]

Reminding everyone of a transcendent dimension requires a new approach among Orthodox Christians, His All-Holiness suggests. To contribute to the pressing needs of today in the fields of law and human rights, Orthodox churches must reconcile themselves with a basic fact: the human rights of today do not and cannot reflect the wholeness of Christian life and belief. In the postmodern world, Christians are just members of very diverse societies, and cannot claim any cultural, spiritual, political, or legal monopoly.

Bartholomew is aware that, although many political parties and movements still draw their values and inspiration from Christian teachings, and polities keep some connection with their religious roots, new rights-based movements and a growing anti-Christian sentiment have made Christians feel 'marginalised'. However, he does not complain about Christian marginalisation, nor does he reminisce about a sort of golden past in which Christianity was a strong and powerful cultural and political player. As Benedict XVI urged European Christians to conceive of themselves as 'creative minorities',[22] even though the legal, political, and institutional frameworks in Europe still carried visible signs of Christianity, Bartholomew is similarly urging Orthodox Christians not to feel as if they have been cornered. In his words, '[t]he initial sterile collision of Christianity and modernity in the West must on no account be repeated in the encounter of modernity with the Orthodox Church'. Even more poignantly, he states that 'Orthodox Christianity must finally overcome its defensive attitude towards the Enlightenment' that, in Bartholomew's account, was the cradle of modern human rights. 'The spirit of the Enlightenment', His All-Holiness adds, 'is not in itself a threat to our identity'.

The Ecumenical Patriarch invites Orthodoxy to a balanced approach – one that does not repudiate modernity and postmodernity nor embrace them uncritically. He notes that '[l]ike total rejection, total affirmation is not the right attitude towards modernity. A differentiated attitude is required … [O]ne must not confuse the true spirit of the Enlightenment with its distortions'. The Orthodox Church can help contemporary societies sift through the thick layer of human rights that have developed over the centuries, looking for what meets the true material and transcendent needs of human beings.

21 C. Malik, 'The Near East: The Search for Truth', 30 *Foreign Affairs* (1952) 231–264, 264.

22 Benedict XVI, Interview of the Holy Father Benedict XVI During the Flight to the Czech Republic, 26 September 2009, www.vatican.va/content/benedict-xvi/en/speeches/2009/september/documents/hf_ben-xvi_spe_20090926_interview.html

V. Conclusion

His All-Holiness portrays the dynamic between Orthodox Christianity and human rights today as one of tension and possibly cooperation. Above all, he urges proponents of the two traditions to embark on a fruitful process of mutual learning. Bartholomew does not overlook the discrepancies between the two traditions; he actually insists on the historical differences between them, perhaps to a higher degree than what history itself suggests. However, he believes that the gaps between these two logics and cultures can feed each other as long as they reinvent their respective approaches.

Human rights need purification. This process would not make them narrower – it would actually broaden their horizon to include the social component of personhood. Orthodoxy also needs to clarify for itself the difference between its popular component and its nationalistic drift. Moreover, it needs to understand itself as a positive and creative force within a scenario in which it has become just one of many players. In elaborating on the challenges in this way, Bartholomew indirectly shines a light on the logic that pervades the growing Christian dissatisfaction with rights and encourages the development of anti-rights narratives among Christians. Such narratives are a retreat, Bartholomew seems to say: they take life from the widespread perceptions of estrangement and powerlessness among Christians.

However, by developing such narratives, sceptics about rights betray some of the ideals they stand for. Although they argue for stronger social bonds, a more relational understanding of human personhood, and a profound consideration for institutions such as marriage, they actually operate by severing ties and cutting bonds between themselves and the rest of contemporary societies. Those who are mindful of the transcendent nature of human beings and societies at large cannot self-isolate, withdraw from good relationships with their neighbours, and simply push for alternative agendas that sideline rights.

The Ecumenical Patriarch suggests that healing the selective, often self-referential, and ideologically loaded language of rights first requires that Orthodoxy identify why the logic of rights has won the hearts of modern and postmodern societies. The lesson of Bartholomew deserves not just praise but also widespread attention among Christians, well beyond those of the Orthodox persuasion. Rights need healing, not replacement.[23]

23 This chapter has also drawn on A. Pin, 'Balancing Dignity, Equality and Religious Freedom: A Transnational Topic', 19 *Ecclesiastical Law Journal* (2017) 292–306; 'Arab Constitutionalism and Human Dignity', 50 *George Washington International Law Review* (2017) 1–67; 'Christianity and Law in Europe Today', forthcoming in *The Oxford Handbook on Christianity and Law* (J. Witte, Jr and R. Domingo, eds. Oxford: Oxford University Press, 2023).

Address IV
Religious Freedom

Religion and Freedom

(Académie des Sciences Morales et Politiques,
Paris, 28 January 2014)
[originally in French]

…

Among human rights, the right to religious freedom is the greatest challenge for religions, but it also opens positive perspectives for them. The right to religious freedom requires more from the religions than the tolerance of differences, which is not unknown to them. Tolerance has, of course, nothing to do with a nihilistic acceptance of everything, with careless approval of different opinions and indifference to the truth. Openness to difference presupposes trust in one's own religion, certainty about one's value, self-esteem, inner strength, and sincere respect for one's tradition. Whoever does not respect his own tradition is not able to appreciate and respect the traditions of others.

Also, with the word 'tolerance' comes a sense of superiority over the other. This does not only refer to the attitude of a majority towards a minority, but it is also possible to be expressed by a minority towards the many, as long as this minority considers that it owns the truth.

Indeed, the stakes in properly approaching religious freedom is the way by which truth and the relationship with the truth are understood. It is important to recognise that the boundaries between truth and untruth do not coincide with the boundaries of our religion and the religion of the other. This admission does not, naturally, include relativism and theological minimalism.

The truth of religion cannot be separated from the truth of human freedom. God is the God of man. This means that an essential criterion of the truth of religion is whether it respects and protects human dignity. His Eminence the Metropolitan of Pergamon, John Zizioulas, writes: 'No religious faith justifies its existence solely by claiming that it possesses

DOI: 10.4324/9781032636740-11

the truth. It must show that it exists not to enslave, but to liberate man, to respond to his deepest existential problems'.[1]

An obstacle to the correct understanding of the content of the universal right of religious freedom is also the opinion that it is about securing an individual-centred right, linked to Western civilisation and corrosive to non-Western traditions. Such a theory is an injustice to human rights, as in the classic French *Déclaration des droits de l'homme et du citoyen* of 1789, there were already manifestations of the three principles of the French Revolution, *Liberté–Égalité–Fraternité*. It is characteristic that the three above principles are also named in the first article of the Universal Declaration of Human Rights of 1948. 'All human beings are born free and equal in dignity and rights. They are endowed with reason and conscience and should act towards one another in a spirit of brotherhood'.

This internal connection of liberty, equality and fraternity is hidden today when these three principles are associated with one of the so-called 'three generations' of human rights, or with liberalism and socialism. The classic rights of the first generation are not only rights of freedom but, at the same time, are rights of equality and solidarity. The economic and social rights of the 'second generation' do not only guarantee equality but are equally rights of freedom. The same is true for 'third generation' rights, such as the right to development, which expresses the initial dynamic focus of the human rights movement, so long as freedom and equality remain decisive elements for the concept of development.[2]

...

In this sense, in relation to the right to religious freedom, the following apply: If the three principles of liberty, equality, and fraternity or solidarity are interrelated and interpreted alongside one another given that each right must also correspond to these three principles, then freedom of religion cannot, as an individual right, be the privilege of a few but must apply to everyone equally and must at the same time enable the formation of communities ... Freedom of religion is properly understood only in relation to equality and fraternity or solidarity. This proves that human rights should not be understood as abstract principles, but as rights of specific people, who co-exist and are mutually dependent. It also makes clear that solidarity belongs at the core of political and social life, since it highlights the deepest meaning of freedom and equality, freedom within equality and equality within the framework of freedom.

1. John Zizioulas, 'Ἀλήθεια, Ἀνεκτικότητα καί Μονοθεϊσμός. Εἶναι δυνατός ἕνας διαθρησκειακός διάλογος;' ['Truth, Toleration and Monotheism. Is an Inter-religious dialogue posible?'] 84 *Θεολογία* [*Theology*] (2013) 5–9, at 8.
2. B. H. Bielefeldt, *Philosophie der Menschenrechte. Grundlagen eines weltweiten Freiheitsethos* (Darmstadt, 1998) 92–93.

An objection of Orthodoxy in relation to the right of religious freedom concerns the position of the Church in the modern secular state. Fears are expressed that the Church is in danger of being marginalised ... Another obstacle is the suspicion of the Orthodox that the acceptance of the model in question will lead to the westernisation of Church and State relations in the Orthodox world.

The Orthodox Churches are today faced with the challenge of building a 'new cooperation' (*synallelia*) with the modern state, which will save the well-known spirit of *synergeia* of Church and State from the Byzantine tradition, that is, of the shared service of the human person. The institutional separation of Church and State and their distinct roles are in place to ensure both identity and cooperation of the two parties in all matters of common interest. This appears to be a solution that respects the right to religious freedom, just as the biblical spirit of 'render to Caesar the things that are Caesar's and to God the things that are God's' (Matthew 22:21) also proves that the modern state of law in the world is not in itself a threat to the Church and does not reject religious culture.

...

We believe that the protection of religious freedom by the modern state of law, which ensures the fundamental conditions of the varieties of religious expression and the social presence of religious communities, makes the dialogue of religions possible and imperative. This dialogue frees religions from introversion which usually feeds prejudices against the different, contributes to the discovery and promotion of religions' common humanistic assumptions and acts as a bulwark against fundamentalism.

...

What is required of Orthodoxy is to function as a positive challenge for modern man, as a proposal of relational freedom, as a 'culture of personhood' and as a 'culture of solidarity' within the globalised modern or post-modern civilisation, which has offered humanity many invaluable gifts. However, it seems that it closes man to himself and his individual happiness. Our strength is the Cross and the Resurrection of Christ, the revelation of the Truth as Love, the foundation and horizon of our freedom, which is 'relationship' and not 'possession'.

7 An Eastern Orthodox Approach to Religious Freedom

Isidoros C. Katsos[1]

Is there *one* Orthodox position on human rights and religious freedom? The simple answer is 'No!' While Orthodox Christian leaders and communities cherish human rights language because of its self-evident utility for the Orthodox Church as a religious minority in the West, an elite few among the most well-known Orthodox theologians objects to the modern language of human rights because of its alleged individualistic moral agenda. The gulf between theory and practice resulted in a well-known ambivalent stance of Orthodox Christianity towards human rights. In other words, it must be understood from the outset that there is not one but several conflicting Orthodox views on the issue of human rights.[2] This ambivalent stance appears to have come to a happy end with the adoption of an *official* position of the Orthodox Church in the Holy and Great Council held in Crete in June 2016. §16 of the Encyclical of the Holy and Great Council now recognises religious freedom 'in all its aspects' as 'a fundamental human right'.[3] This recognition is glossed by 'nuanced' language:

> The approach to human rights on the part of the Orthodox Church centers on the danger of individual rights falling into individualism and a culture of 'rights'.

Underneath the concern for individualism, however, hides a recognisable shift in attitude. Human rights are no longer considered *intrinsically*

1 In preparing this chapter, I was supported by my participation as Senior Fellow in the 'Orthodoxy and Human Rights' project, sponsored by Fordham University's Orthodox Christian Studies Center and generously funded by the Henry Luce Foundation and Leadership 100.

2 The doctrinal controversy is expertly documented and discussed in A. Papanikolaou, *The Mystical as Political: Democracy and Non-Radical Orthodoxy* (Notre Dame, IN: University of Notre Dame Press, 2012) 87–130; P. Ladouceur, *Modern Orthodox Theology: Behold, I Make All Things New* (London: T&T Clark, 2019) 253–262.

3 Publicly accessible at www.holycouncil.org/encyclical-holy-council (last accessed: June 2023). All citations are from the internet edition.

DOI: 10.4324/9781032636740-12

individualistic; rather, it is only the *danger* of individualism that is denounced by the Orthodox Church, not individual rights as such.

In this chapter, I will show that the shift in attitude was first signalled by His All Holiness the Ecumenical Patriarch Bartholomew I in a lecture on 'Religion and Freedom' delivered at the Académie des Sciences Morales et Politiques in Paris in 2014 (from now on: 'lecture'). The Holy and Great Council thus gave official expression to the Ecumenical Patriarch's view two years later. I will then argue that the view of the Patriarch on religious freedom is confronted with deep-rooted antinomies in Orthodox identity and history. A superficial reading of the Patriarch's lecture suggests that religious freedom poses a challenge for the Orthodox Church in a pluralistic world. A careful reading, however, reveals that, if brought to light, the inherited antinomies can be resolved from within the intellectual resources of the Orthodox Church. In this reading of the Patriarch's view, pluralism is already embedded in the church's teaching on human dignity and freedom.

I. The Patriarchal Lecture: Locating Religious Freedom

The Paris lecture of the Ecumenical Patriarch signalled a pivotal moment in the Orthodox discourse on human rights. Until then, the views of Orthodox Church leaders remained ambivalent, while the position of the Orthodox Church at large remained obscure. Previous attempts to endorse human rights language at the official level of the church included the 'Basic' Teaching of the Russian Orthodox Church 'On Human Dignity, Freedom, and Human Rights', published in 2008.[4] It soon became clear, however, that the letter of the Russian 'Basic Teaching' was animated by a spirit of deep insecurity about the effects of libertarian freedom on ethical matters to which the Russian Church felt strongly opposed (most notably, gay rights and abortion legislation).[5] The double standard of the Russian 'Basic Teaching' ('yes' to rights in the context of the symphony

4 Russian Orthodox Church, *The Russian Orthodox Church's Basic Teaching on Human Dignity, Freedom and Rights* (Department for External Church Relations of the Russian Orthodox Church, 2010). Curiously, the document is no longer available online in the English website of the Russian Orthodox Church (https://mospat.ru/en). It is still available online at https://nanovic.nd.edu/assets/17001/seminar_ii_russian_ orth_church.pdf or at http://orthodoxrights.org/documents/russian-church-freedom-and-rights (last accessed: June 2023).

5 See the illuminating study of K. Stoeckl, *The Russian Orthodox Church and Human Rights* (London: Routledge, 2014). On the strong convictions of the Russian Church on sexual ethics see section II of the *Basic Teaching*.

between church and state, but 'no' in the case of disagreement)[6] did not help clarify the Orthodox view on libertarian freedom. In fact, it obscured it further. In delivering his Paris lecture, the question was whether the Ecumenical Patriarch had anything new to say. I here argue that he did.

The lecture commences with a brief reflection on the conceptual origins of religious freedom which can be traced back to the Edict of Milan in 313 CE. It then turns to the modern humanistic tradition and the birth of religious freedom as a human right, culminating in Article 18 of the Universal Declaration of Human Rights. The lecture contends that religious freedom as a human right entails religious pluralism, which, in turn, creates a challenge for every religion with exclusive claims to truth. It then suggests that the challenge of pluralism must be overcome from within the conceptual tools of every religion. As regards Orthodox Christianity, the conceptual tools required to overcome the challenge of pluralism are relationality and freedom as key features of the signature Orthodox doctrine of transcendental personalism.

Orthodox personalism conceptualises human dignity and freedom in its communitarian and existential dimensions. The latter is incompatible with the individualistic interpretation of religious freedom, which must be criticised and rejected. This does not mean, however, that there are no alternative interpretations which are compatible with the Orthodox personalist view of freedom. The lecture sketches such an alternative interpretation by situating religious freedom in a communitarian-participatory framework. Libertarian freedom in its personalist interpretation requires the concept of 'social justice', further analysable into two principles: the principle of 'equality' as communitarian complement to libertarian freedom, and the principle of 'solidarity', which provides the required participatory framework for both freedom and equality to unfold. Solidarity 'highlights the deepest meaning of freedom and equality, freedom within equality and equality within the framework of freedom'. The Ecumenical Patriarch argues therefore for a conception of libertarian freedom within a 'culture of solidarity' as the secular version of the 'culture of personhood' or 'relational freedom' advocated by the church. From within a culture of solidarity, then, there is nothing incompatible between the fundamental principles of Orthodox anthropology and human rights. On the contrary, modern humanism can even become a positive impetus for religion. 'Personally', the Patriarch suggests, 'we consider that an encounter

6 For example, see section III of the *Basic Teaching*: 'Human rights cannot be superior to the values of the spiritual world ... Not a divine institution, human rights should not come into conflict with the Divine Revelation ... The development and implementation of the human rights concept should be harmonized with the norms of morality, with the ethical principle laid down by God in human nature and discernible in the voice of conscience'.

between Orthodoxy and the Enlightenment can serve as a trigger for Orthodox theology to promote both its humanistic principles and freedom as a basic notion of its anthropology'.

I suggest that the argument of the lecture is novel compared to previous arguments about Orthodoxy and human rights. The novelty consists of a shift in the epistemic stance of the Orthodox Church towards secular humanism. As already mentioned, leading Orthodox thinkers, followed by conservative church leaders, suspect the humanist tradition of being *inherently* individualistic, therefore inherently anti-personalist and anti-Orthodox. By contrast, the lecture argues carefully for the genuine compatibility of human rights with the Orthodox view of human dignity. On the one hand, the traditional nuanced language is preserved. Human rights must be approached dialectically:

> Religions can adopt the humanistic dimensions and advances of modernity and at the same time criticise its negative and extreme manifestations ...

On the other hand, the concerns of critics of rights are straightforwardly addressed and opposed:

> Of course, religions are not allowed, by invoking this lack of clarity regarding the content and limits of human rights as a pretext, to devalue them or even reject them.

The opposition also extends to particularly Orthodox concerns about the alleged anti-communitarian nature of human rights:

> Both the individual-centred view of human rights, as well as the emphasis on the primacy of the community ... contain misconceptions ... Human rights are not directed against the community, but against its absolutisation. By protecting the individual, they neither reject the community nor do they defend individualism and autonomism.

The Patriarchal critique signifies a significant shift in the church's attitude towards rights. Human rights are no longer rejected *as such* as anti-communitarian and individualistic. Only *one interpretation* of rights is denounced as incoherent, namely their individualistic interpretation. If freedom is decoupled from solidarity, i.e. from the secular expression of the communitarian ideal, freedom becomes individualistic and is no longer able to provide a life of *koinōnia* or *sobornost* as a necessary condition for human fulfilment. The individualistic decoupling of freedom from solidarity is, however, not the only possible interpretation of human rights. In fact, it is not even a correct interpretation. Rights ought not to be conceived independently of their egalitarian and participatory framework, the Patriarch argues. If they do, they fail to fulfil their ultimate purpose which is to provide justice for all

The Patriarch's critique is not addressed against rights but only against a certain misconception of them. It is a critique of the transmutation of the *rights of the individual* into *individualist rights.* As we will see in the following section, this is not a critique voiced from without the culture of rights but from within. Contrary to the Russian 'Basic Teaching', which expects the Orthodox to ignore human rights in case of conflicting moral agendas, the Ecumenical Patriarch expects the Orthodox to defend rights even at their worst. It is the task of the church to work together with secularism to bring back libertarian freedom to its proper meaning instead of abandoning rights to their individualistic misinterpretations and misconceptions. To defend rights from misinterpretations promotes critical reflection and cultural dialogue; to ignore rights due to disagreement leads to cultural war. The epistemic difference is huge.

II. Religious Freedom As A Challenge – Or Not

So far, we have seen religious freedom through the lens of the general argument of the Patriarch's lecture. This conforms with the logic of human rights. Religious freedom exemplifies libertarian freedom in its intersection with religion. Since the individualistic interpretation of libertarian freedom is incoherent, the same applies to religious freedom as a sub-specimen of freedom. In the words of the Patriarch:

> An obstacle to the correct understanding of the content of the universal right of religious freedom is also the opinion that it is about securing an individual-centred right, linked to Western civilisation and corrosive to non-Western traditions. Such a theory is an injustice to human rights …

As the lecture turns specifically to 'the right of religious freedom', it considers it to be 'the greatest challenge for religions'. The reader should not be alarmed. Here too, religious freedom functions as an exemplary case of human rights. According to the Patriarch:

> human rights are among the most challenging issues that have ever been posed to religions.

Why is this so? To answer the question, we need to dig deeper into the lecture's subtext and context. It is there that we discover a series of inherited antinomies to which the Patriarch alludes even though he does not fully spell them out.

A persisting historical antinomy concerns the constantly shifting legal status of the Orthodox Church as a religious community.[7] The passage from Rome to Byzantium was marked by the passage from a religion of the persecuted to a religion of the persecutors. Recent scholarship contests the length of Roman persecutions, their exclusive anti-Christian nature, and the actual number of Christian martyrs.[8] It does not deny, however, that before Constantine Christianity was more on the side of the oppressed, while after Theodosius it shifted more to the side of the oppressor. As a rule, the church leaders did not have the institutional power or the authority to enforce the law. They could not suppress, persecute, torture, or exile their opponents by themselves. Anti-pagan, anti-Jewish, and anti-heretic policies belonged to the exclusive power of the state. Gradually, however, all state officials had to be members of the church – officially at least.[9] They were never accused of sinning while pursuing religious prohibitions. Importantly, for schismatics to become the target of imperial punishment, they first had to be cut off from the church. That was the role of local bishops and of synods. Not only the active participation of the church, but also its silence, *enabled* state violence.

With the passage from Byzantium to the reign of Islam, the church in the East reverted back to the position of the oppressed, enjoying the lesser legal status of a religious minority. With the birth of the modern national state in the 19th century, the church in the Balkans enjoyed on several occasions the privileged status of the official religion of the land. Throughout its long history, the church in the East revolved around a constant dialectic of being-in-power and suffering-under-power. The birth of modern human rights came at the cost of a confused identity on the part of the Orthodox Church: was it historically on the side of the beneficiaries or on the side of the violators of religious freedom? The

7 In what follows, I develop further my views first expressed in 'Religionsfreiheit – Orthodoxe Sicht' (Rahmenartikel) [Framework Article on Religious Freedom from an Orthodox Perspective, in German] in T. Meckel, H. Hallermann, M. Droege, and H. de Wall, eds., *Lexikon für Kirchen- und Religionsrecht*, vol. 3 (Leiden: Brill, 2020) 874–876.

8 See C. Moss, *The Myth of Persecution: How Early Christians Invented a Story of Martyrdom* (New York, NY: HarperCollins, 2013).

9 See Theodosius II, *Novella* 3; text and commentary in A. Linder, *The Jews in Roman Imperial Legislation* (Detroit, MI: Wayne State University Press, 1987) 323–337. On religious prohibitions in Byzantium see J. Witte, 'The right to freedom of religion: An historical perspective from the West' in S. Ferrari, M. Hill, A.A. Jamal, and R. Bottoni, eds., *Routledge Handbook of Freedom of Religion or Belief* (Abingdon: Routledge, 2021) 11–26 (esp. 12–14); D. Baudy, 'Prohibitions of Religion in Antiquity: Setting the Course of Europe's Religious History' in C. Ando and J. Rüpke, eds., *Religion and Law in Classical and Christian Rome* (Stuttgart: Franz Steiner Verlag, 2006) 100–114.

simple fact is that it has been on both sides – and that it remains so. In Russia, Greece, and other Balkan states, Orthodoxy enjoys a privileged legal status. At the same time, in the neighbouring Turkey the Ecumenical Patriarchate struggles against the restrictions of Turkish law. The constant shift in the legal status of the Orthodox Church between majority and minority religion generates confusion about where it stands with regard to religious freedom. The Patriarch alludes to this antinomical shift in the opening paragraphs of his lecture noting that 'the Edict of Milan marks the beginning of the end of the long-lasting, unmerciful persecutions against Christians'. A few paragraphs later he continues:

> the emergence of Christianity as *religio imperii* created problems for the Church itself and bequeathed 'strong temptations' of authoritarian imposition in the centuries that followed.

Behind the antinomy of the legal status hides the antinomy of the church as both spiritual and political institution, hence as an *institution of power*. Religious freedom as a human right aims to protect all forms of religious expression against institutions of power, the first among which is traditionally the state. As a religious community, the Orthodox Church is the beneficiary of religious freedom. Yet, the church often functions as an institution of power, deeply embedded in the political ideology of the state. For example, this has been the case of the Byzantine *symphonia* model of mutual support and cooperation between church and state or the modern *Christian nation* model of a national state-supported church. Every time that the church functions in theory or in practice as an institution of power, its actions must be measured against the backdrop of religious freedom. The deep antinomy between the self-understanding of the Orthodox Church as both spiritual and political institutions turns religious freedom and human rights into a real challenge. When the church functions as a power institution, it clashes with religious freedom. When it functions as a spiritual institution, it calls upon religious freedom. Since the church functions as a bit of both in many countries, it is truly challenging for the church leaders to strike the right balance.

Because of this authoritarian aspect of the church, some Orthodox tend to denounce the Byzantine model of state–church synergy. This view is paradigmatically expressed in the *Social Ethos Document*, approved by the Holy and Sacred Council of the Ecumenical Patriarchate in January 2020. §13 of the *Document* contends that:

> … the dissolution of the ancient compact between state and church – or throne and altar – has also been a great blessing for Christian culture. It has freed the church from what was all too frequently a

> slavish and unholy submission to earthly power and a complicity in its evils.

Meanwhile, revisionary scholarship has challenged the idea of a church slavishly submitting to the state under the Byzantine *symphonia* model. On this view:

> *symphonia* meant a harmony of powers whose very juxtaposition delineated precise limits of power: to each their own, and from each their proper sphere of accountability ... *Symphonia* ... meant exactly what it stated: two differently sounding agendas, a political and a religious-ecclesiastic, constantly seeking to broker balance. *Symphonia* does not, and never did, mean the church went hand-in-hand with the state.[10]

According to this view, the model of *symphonia* is better understood as a system of checks and balances between the church and the state. Checks and balances between institutions of power are, of course, the essence of human rights with judicial control. Under the modern rule of law, human rights are meant to counter-balance abuse of power in all aspects of social and political life. Religious freedom as a human right is thus a principle of balance of power and control of abuse in the domain of religion. This is exactly what the model of *symphonia* aimed at, according to the view of revisionary scholarship. If we follow this view, the image that emerges is no longer that of 'slavish submission', but of a church functioning as a spiritual institution with the power to counter-balance the abuse of state power in a cultural milieu of religious and social pluralism.[11] Hence the conclusion:

> It is thus wholly disingenuous to speak of human rights issues as if somehow they are not part of the fundamental fabric of Orthodoxy's ancient constitution.[12]

How far can one take this view? The revisionary scholarship certainly allows for a critical re-examination of the theological roots of libertarian

10 J. McGuckin, 'The Issue of Human Rights in Byzantium and the Orthodox Christian Tradition', in J. Witte and F. Alexander, eds., *Christianity and Human Rights: An Introduction* (Cambridge: Cambridge University Press, 2011) 173–190 (esp. 175).

11 On religious pluralism in the Roman Empire see J. Rüpke, *From Jupiter to Christ: On the History of Religion in the Roman Imperial Period* (Oxford: Oxford University Press, 2014) 185–209.

12 J. McGuckin, 'The Issue of Human Rights in Byzantium', 180.

freedom in the Orthodox tradition. A few programmatic studies suggest that the conceptual origins of libertarian freedom can be traced back to the early Christian patristic literature. Even though patristic thought 'did not result in a fully developed articulation of freedom in terms of human rights, dignity, and social justice', the early Christian literature is permeated by a theological grammar of pluralistic freedom.[13]

The Ecumenical Patriarch in his Paris lecture understands religious pluralism as an open call to every religion. Religions 'are invited to understand that human rights function in favour of pluralism'; 'human rights enshrine the foundational conditions and terms of cultural difference and of interculturalism'. In a pluralistic framework, the Patriarch suggests, no religion has exclusive claims on truth: '… an essential criterion of the truth of religion is whether it respects and protects human dignity'. This is huge. Instead of theorising human rights according to the theological standards of the Orthodox Church, the Patriarch invites us to imagine the Orthodox Church being measured according to the standards of human rights. Gone is the traditional divide between 'Orthodoxy and heresy'. Introduced is pluralistic religious freedom as the criterion of the church's truth. Quoting the words of the Elder Metropolitan of Pergamon, the late John Zizioulas, the Ecumenical Patriarch affirms:

> No religious faith justifies its existence solely by claiming that it possesses the truth. It must show that it exists not to enslave, but to liberate man, to respond to his deepest existential problems.

In a most kenotic moment, every religion, whether Orthodox or not, is subordinated to human dignity and freedom as a universal criterion of truth. Freedom is theorised in existential and relational terms. It is the truth that liberates every human being from the yoke of individualism – in Christian terms: from the yoke of our fallen condition. Orthodoxy is thus measured against the backdrop of human rights, but only because human rights can be theorised from the backdrop of a transcendental personalist philosophy. The Patriarchal critique of Orthodoxy from within religious freedom becomes the converse side of the Patriarchal critique of human rights from within the Orthodox tradition. Both critiques aim at a non-individualistic, egalitarian, and participatory notion of human dignity and freedom, whether in its humanistic or its Orthodox expression.

13 See E. Prodromou, 'Orthodox Christian Contributions to Freedom: Historical Foundations, Contemporary Problematics' in T. Shah and A. Hertzke, eds., *Christianity and Freedom*, vol. 1: *Historical Perspectives* (Cambridge: Cambridge University Press, 2016) 305–311.

III. Conclusion

Starting from the deep antinomies of the historic self-understanding of the Orthodox Church as an institution between state power and existential freedom, the Ecumenical Patriarch gently invites the audience of his Paris lecture to take a leap of faith outside and beyond the comfort zone of doctrinal complacency. Instead of looking at religious freedom through the lens of Orthodoxy, the Patriarch invites his audience to contemplate Orthodoxy through the lens of human dignity and freedom. For those who cling to a romantic but dated narrative of a harmonious synergy between church and state, religious freedom will continue to pose a tremendous challenge to the church's self-understanding as a powerful institution. Libertarian freedom becomes, on this view, a dimension of the ambiguity of being an Orthodox in a pluralistic world. For those, however, who are ready to re-examine the intellectual resources of the Eastern Orthodox Church in the light of revisionary scholarship, the Patriarch's appeal to religious freedom contains the solution to the ambiguities inherited from the past.

The theological anthropology of the church never theorised the human person independently of freedom. Similarly, the *symphonia* model was never meant to serve institutional power but, instead, to counterbalance it through spiritual authority. It is the paradoxical authority of the human weakness of the Cross glorified by the unseen light of resurrection. In the sacrificial light of the Cross, the correct self-understanding of the church necessarily entails the protection of human dignity and freedom against all forms of violence and oppression. In its existentialist, patristic, interpretation, freedom is understood in relational terms, as ontological freedom. Anything that opposes it is deemed incompatible, not with the church, but with the meaning of being human. 'Humanism' and 'pluralism' thus signify the conceptual space of deliberate self-criticism of the Orthodox Church against any abuse of spiritual authority from within. At the crossroads of Orthodoxy and human rights, the Ecumenical Patriarch suggests, lies the ambiguity of the human person in all its tragic destiny and glory. It is the ambiguity of libertarian freedom in its twofold interpretation: personalistic or individualistic.

8 Ecumenical Approaches to Religious Freedom

Mark Hill KC[1]

Commentators have long debated the extent to which the drafters of international instruments, like the Universal Declaration of Human Rights (1948),[2] drew upon Judaeo-Christian concepts when framing a suite of inter-dependent rights regimes, pre-eminent among them freedom of religion. In his address on Religion and Freedom, His All-Holiness was entirely comfortable in bridging the passage of time between these post-war iterations (his starting point) and the Edict of Milan which he identifies as a 'pivotal moment' some 1700 years before.[3] Whilst this chapter gives primacy to the consideration of religious freedom, seen through the lens of the regulatory and other normative instruments of Christian churches, it begins – as it must – with a voyage upstream, to the people, philosophies and events which led to this repository of international instruments and their comprehensive statements of freedom of religion.

I. Foundations of Freedom of Religion

Religious liberty, as understood today, undoubtedly originates in ancient Jewish constructions of covenant and *mitzvot*, and classic Christian concepts of *ius* and *libertas*, freedom and covenant.[4] It is oversimplification to claim a linear progression from Judaeo-Christian concepts of dignity, respect, and sanctity of human life, to current understandings of religious

1 This chapter draws on the author's contribution to the *Oxford Handbook on Christianity and Law* (forthcoming), entitled 'Christianity and Human Rights Law' which in turn relies on N. Doe, 'Religious Freedom: Christian Perspectives', in S. Ferrari, M. Hill, A. Jamal, and R. Bottoni, eds., *Routledge Handbook of Freedom of Religion or Belief* (Abingdon: Routledge, 2021) 88–101.

2 See also the European Convention on Human Rights; Charter of the Organisation of American States and the American Convention on Human Rights; and African Charter on Human and Peoples' Rights.

3 'Religion and Freedom' a lecture delivered on 28 January 2014 at the *Académie des Sciences Morales et Politiques* in Paris.

4 J. Witte, 'Introduction', in J. Witte and F.S. Alexander, eds., *Christianity and Human Rights: An Introduction* (Cambridge: Cambridge University Press, 2011) 12.

DOI: 10.4324/9781032636740-13

liberty, framed in international treaties which inherit much of their texture and colour from belief systems of previous generations. Christianity has long been a transmitter of morality and ethics, but so also have the other Abrahamic faiths and world religions. The universality of modern regimes protects fundamental rights, including religious freedom, for everybody equally, whereas from medieval times, through the Reformation, the Enlightenment and beyond, the emphasis was generally on embedding freedom of religion for a particular faith group or denomination, whilst at the same time persecuting – or at least disadvantaging – those adhering to other beliefs. The phrase freedom of religion (*libertas religionis*) was reputedly introduced into Western Christian thought by Tertullian of Carthage (c. 160–220), a theologian and lawyer who lived in North Africa. After decrying the Roman persecution of Christians, he wrote:

> It is only just and a privilege inherent in human nature that every person should be able to worship according to his own convictions; the religious practice of one person neither harms nor helps another. It is not part of religion to coerce religious practice, for it is by choice not coercion that we should be led to religion.

The Edict of Milan (313) for the first time guaranteed to Christians, alongside all other faiths, 'a public and free liberty to practise their religion or cult' and 'free permission to follow their own religion and worship as befits the peacefulness of our times'. The Edict also recognised the rights of Christian groups to own property and places of worship, and the right to restitution of properties confiscated in earlier times of persecution. But despite its lofty ambitions, the Edict led to the persecution of Jews, pagans, apostates and heretics, ending in a further imperial Edict in 380 legally establishing Trinitarian Christianity.[5] In like fashion, the myth of Magna Carta as declaring the freedom of the English Church and embodying fundamental freedoms lives on; the reality of this and other medieval charters of rights was that they advantaged the Christian governing elite, whilst heretics, Jews, Muslims, or the Orthodox had no protection.[6] But it was Alcuin of York, scholar, cleric, and advisor to Emperor Charlemagne (747–814), who counselled that 'faith arises from the will, not from compulsion ... you can persuade a man to believe, but you

5 For a fuller exposition of these events, see J. Witte, 'The Right to Freedom of Religion: An Historical Perspective from the West' in S. Ferrari, et al., *Routledge Handbook on Freedom of Religion or Belief*, op. cit., Ch. 1.

6 R. Helmholz, 'Magna Carta and the Law of Nations' in R. Griffith-Jones and M. Hill, eds., *Magna Carta, Religion and the Rule of Law* (Cambridge: Cambridge University Press, 2015) Ch. 5.

cannot force him', to dissuade Frankish kings from the forced conversion of pagans.[7] Even Augustine of Hippo (354–430) campaigned against the schismatic Donatists in North Africa. Restrictions were placed on public worship by Jews throughout the Holy Roman Empire, though some, including Pope Gregory the Great (590–604), censured forced conversion to Christianity. Medieval popes Callistus II and Innocent III forbade that Jews suffer prejudice and violence, whilst the Dominican priest Bartolome de Las Casas, was highly critical of the Spanish authorities in compelling the conversion of Amerindians to Catholicism.

But since the middle of the last century, and coinciding with the codification of human rights regimes, there has been a discernible rise in religious pluralism, secularism and humanism, and accordingly, our exploration now turns to how religious freedom is understood by Christians.

II. Christian Understandings of Religious Freedom

For Christians, freedom of religion is essential to faith, because, in the words of the World Council of Churches, 'God's redemptive dealing with men is not coercive'.[8] The Roman Catholic Church has a rich concept of religious liberty. *Dignitatis humanae*, the Second Vatican Council Declaration on Religious Liberty (1965) places religious freedom within traditional Church teaching on human dignity. It is the cornerstone of a society that promotes human dignity and is fundamental to human flourishing. It requires the State to help create conditions for religion to flourish and, as humans are social beings, religious liberty also has an associational element, according self-governance to religious institutions. Accordingly, 'religious freedom [should] be everywhere provided with an effective constitutional guarantee and respect be shown for the high duty and right of man freely to lead his religious life in society'.[9]

The Anglican Communion has a less sophisticated account, although the Lambeth Conference endorses the Universal Declaration of Human Rights, asserting 'each person's freedom of thought, conscience and religion' as an 'absolute right'.[10] The laws of member churches do not directly address human rights. However, the *Principles of Canon Law*

7 N.R. Needham, *2,000 Years of Christ's Power: The Middle Ages* (Grace Publications, 2000).

8 'Statement on Religious Liberty', in the New Delhi Report: The Third Assembly of the World Council of Churches 1961 (New York, 1962) 159.

9 *Dignitatis Humanae*, 4–5, 15.

10 For Lambeth Conference 1998 statements, see N. Doe, 'Canonical Approaches to Human Rights in Anglican Churches', M. Hill, ed., *Religious Liberty and Human Rights* (Cardiff: University of Wales Press, 2002) 185.

Common to the Churches of the Anglican Communion (2022) recognise two types of right – inherent and acquired:

> all persons, equal in dignity before God, have inherent rights and duties inseparable from their dignity as human beings created in the image and likeness of God and called to salvation through Jesus Christ.[11]

And all the faithful enjoy such rights to government, ministry, teaching, worship, sacraments, rites, and property as may flow from their human dignity, baptism, others' duties, and the law of a church.[12]

The United Methodist Church too acknowledges 'all persons as equally valuable in the sight of God' each with 'inherent dignity'; and it asserts 'the right of all religions and their adherents to freedom from legal, economic, and social discrimination'.[13] The law of the Presbyterian Church in Ireland warns against constraining anyone's religious beliefs or invading their rights of conscience. Similarly, in 2017, the General Council of the World Baptist Alliance saw religious freedom as 'a gift of God to all people', regardless of denomination or religion; and it committed itself to the terms of Article 18 of the Universal Declaration of Human Rights.[14]

III. Christians as Advocates of Religious Freedom

Christian churches frequently assert for themselves a corporate right or duty to advocate religious liberty, or they exhort such advocacy from their members. Roman Catholic canon law asserts:

> The Church has the right always and everywhere to proclaim moral principles, even in respect of the social order, and to make judgments about any human matter in so far as this is required by fundamental human rights or the salvation of souls.[15]

However, there is no specific canonical duty to promote religious liberty in society. By way of contrast, the Lambeth Conference 1998 spoke of the

11 *Principles of Canon Law Common to the Churches of the Anglican Communion* (Second edition, 2022), Principle 26.1–2.

12 Ibid., Principle 26.7.

13 United Methodist Church in Northern Europe and Eurasia: Book of Discipline, pars. 103, 121, 161, 162, 164.

14 General Council: Bangkok, Thailand, 5–7 July 2017.

15 *Codex Iuris Canonici* (Code of Canon Law) 1983, c. 747.2.

responsibility of Anglicans as advocates of religious liberty; it called on 'all faith communities, especially the Christian Church, to acknowledge our responsibility to mobilise our spiritual, moral and material resources' to promote it. It also called on 'governments of all the nations our Churches represent to strive for the creation of just and free conditions for people of all religions' to practise beliefs freely.[16]

Similarly, the constitution of the Lutheran World Federation imposes a duty on the Federation to promote human rights.[17] A *Council Statement on Religious Freedom* in 2013 called upon its member churches and the ecumenical community: to strengthen their commitment to freedom of religion; to cooperate in promoting and defending it in their societies and internationally; and to intercede with State and religious authorities to defend individuals or groups whose religious freedoms are curtailed.[18] Further, United Methodist Church law has requirements: to defend religious freedom; to combat acts of hate or violence based on religious affiliation; to support policies that ensure the right of every religious group to exercise its faith free from legal, political, social or economic restriction and discrimination.

The doctrines of Orthodox Christianity merit comment, as they are less frequently referenced in Western literature. As Bartholomew observes:

> Unfortunately, the Orthodox Church is often accused of neglecting the world for the sake of spiritual life, of being centred on worship and liturgy and ignoring social problems, of turning solely towards the future, to the Kingdom of God to come, disregarding the present and the current challenges. Nevertheless, the Holy and Great Council of the Orthodox Church, which was convened in June 2016 on the island of Crete, proved the opposite. It addressed the main contemporary challenges and named as such: secularization, scientism, individualism, the ecological crisis, globalization, violation of human rights, famine, violence, injustice, military conflicts, religious fundamentalism, the refugee, and migrant crisis and others.[19]

An Orthodox appreciation of religious liberty is predicated upon an understanding of its historical context and the pragmatic political forces underlying its modern articulation. In his Religion and Freedom address,

16 N. Doe, 'Canonical Approaches to Human Rights in Anglican Churches', op. cit., 185 at 187.

17 Constitution, Art. III.

18 Public Statement of Lutheran World Federation, adopted 13–18 June 2013.

19 His All-Holiness Ecumenical Patriarch Bartholomew, 'The Role of the Churches in Today's Europe', College of Europe, Bruges, Belgium: 11 November 2019.

Bartholomew suggests that Orthodox Churches today are faced with the challenge of building a 'new cooperation' (*synallelia*) with the modern State.

On the basis of the legal evidence studied by the Ecumenical Christian Law Panel (such as that summarised above), its *Statement of Principles of Christian Law* (2016),[20] discussed in Chapter 2 of this book, recognised as a principle of Christian law that all humans, having been created in the image of God, share an equality of dignity and fundamental human rights; and affirmed that Christian churches should protect and defend human rights for all people in society.[21]

IV. Freedom of Religion as a Means of Ecumenism

The ecumenical movement exists to pursue greater visible unity between Christian churches. The laws of most churches carry a duty to engage in ecumenism on the basis of their belonging to the Church universal,[22] but does ecumenical collaboration extend to promoting religious freedom in civil society? The World Council of Churches has issued a number of documents on religious freedom which show how it may also serve as an instrument of ecumenism. The *Declaration on Religious Liberty*, adopted at its First Assembly in 1948, states:

> An essential element in a good international order is freedom of religion. This is an implication of the Christian faith and of the world-wide nature of Christianity. Christians, therefore, view … religious freedom as an international problem. They are concerned that [it] be everywhere secured. In pleading for [it], they do not ask for any privilege to be granted to Christians that is denied to others.[23]

As its Preamble states, religious freedom must be recognised and observed for all persons without distinction as to race, colour, sex, language, or religion. The Declaration offers four distinct rights, clearly drawn from secular international human rights instruments, emergent then, that is:

20 See M. Hill and N. Doe, 'Principles of Christian Law', 19 *Ecclesiastical Law Journal* (2017) 138–155.

21 Ibid., principle X.2.

22 N. Doe, *Christian Law: Contemporary Principles* (Cambridge: Cambridge University Press, 2013) 279–284.

23 World Council of Churches' *Declaration on Religious Liberty* (Amsterdam, 1948), Preamble, para 1: https://original.religlaw.org/content/religlaw/documents/wccdecreliglib1948.htm

to determine belief; religious expression; association; and institutional autonomy.

A further document *On Religious Liberty*, adopted by the Third Assembly of the World Council of Churches in 1961, noted that humankind is threatened by many forces which curtail or deny freedom. It declared that there was an urgent need to reinvigorate efforts to ensure that every person has the opportunity for the responsible exercise of religious freedom. It identifies a Christian basis for religious liberty, as 'a distinctive human right based on the inherent dignity and inalienable rights of all members of the human family'. Duties attend the right:

> The freedom with which Christ has set us free calls forth responsibility for the rights of others. The civil freedom which we claim in the name of Christ must be freely available for all to exercise responsibly.

Accordingly, it is the corresponding duty of governments to ensure the exercise of these civil rights without discrimination. It is for the churches in their life and witness, recognising their past failures in this regard, to promote the realisation of religious freedom for all.[24]

In 2003, the World Council of Churches' Commission on International Affairs produced another document, *Religious Freedom and Liberty in the Emerging Context*, on protecting religious freedom as a 'shared obligation: between State and Church, between the churches themselves, between individual Christians and the churches themselves, [and] between Christians and people of other faiths'.[25] The Faith and Order Commission in 2013 expressly declared religious freedom to be one of the fundamental dimensions of human dignity.[26] It can therefore be seen that the task of promoting and supporting human rights laws in civil society, for the benefit of people of all faiths and of none, is key to the ecumenical endeavour. Unity in this common cause has become part of both the content and aim of fully engaged ecumenism.

V. Christians as Beneficiaries of Religious Freedom

Whilst Church and State are independent, they are cooperative guardians of religious freedom. The State fosters collective religious liberty in

24 World Council of Churches 'On Religious Liberty', *Journal of Church and State*, Vol. 5, No. 2 (November 1963) 243–245. For earlier references, see ibid., 1–5.

25 Churches Commission on International Affairs: *Religious Freedom and Liberty in the Emerging Context* (18 December 2003).

26 *Common Vision*, paragraph 60. See also R. Williams, 'Human Rights and Religious Faith', Ecumenical Centre, Geneva, 28 February 2012.

recognising the Church's legal entity status in civil law, itself an expression of its autonomy.[27] For the Roman Catholic Church, there is no authority but from God. The State's role is to defend and promote the common good of civil society. However, in their own domain, the political community and the Church are independent of one another and autonomous but should develop a mutual cooperation in favour of the welfare of all.[28] Canon law itself recognises the qualified applicability of State law to the Church:

> When the law of the Church remits some issue to the civil law, the latter is to be observed with the same effects in canon law, in so far as it is not contrary to divine law, and provided it is not otherwise stipulated in canon law.[29]

In turn, unjust laws are not binding in conscience.[30] Anglicans broadly share this approach with regard to their view of the State, cooperation with it, the applicability of civil law, recourse to State courts in disputes among the faithful, and deference to the State. Churches assert their own freedom, their institutional autonomy and their separation from the State – but at the same time they cooperate with it and obey its law, unless the faith itself is threatened.

VI. Conflicts between Freedom of Religion and other Human Rights

International treaties such as the Universal Declaration of Human Rights bring together a suite of rights which must be read together. They are mutually supportive but can on occasion come into conflict. Few rights are absolute; most are qualified, though the qualifications are narrowly drawn and must be strictly interpreted. The European Convention on Human Rights has written the qualifications into the text of the rights. Under Article 9(2) freedom to manifest religion is subject only to such limitations as are prescribed by law and are necessary in a democratic society in the interests of public safety, for the protection of public order, health or morals, or for the protection of the rights and freedoms of others. It is for the judiciary, however, to determine whose rights prevail

27 See M. Hill, R. Sandberg, N. Doe and C Grout, ***Religion and Law in the United Kingdom: Great Britain*** (Kluwer, 3rd edition, 2021).

28 Catechism of the Catholic Church (1994): pars. 1918–1924, 1927; GS 26, 74, 76.

29 Code of Canon Law, c. 22; see e.g. cc. 98 and 110: guardians/adoption; c. 1284: property; c. 1290: secular contract law.

30 Catechism of the Catholic Church (1994): pars. 1897–1942; GS 29–31.

when there is a conflict. Useful interpretative tools, such as the *Punta del Este Declaration on Human Dignity for Everyone Everywhere* (2018), celebrating the recognition of human dignity at the core of the panoply of human rights instruments, promote the concept of maximising human dignity for all whenever rights come into conflict.

Some examples from the United Kingdom. The parents of some pupils at a State school were prevented from authorising teachers to inflict physical chastisement on their children in accordance with their interpretation of biblical teaching. The Judicial Committee of the House of Lords recognised this interfered with the parents' Article 9 right to manifest their religion, but concluded that the interference was justified. The rights of the child not to be injured prevailed.[31] A Christian couple operating a bed and breakfast business could not limit their customers to married opposite-sex couples as they regarded homosexuality as contrary to Christian doctrine. The Supreme Court held that they had opened their home to the public as a business and could not discriminate in providing services on the grounds of sexual orientation, irrespective of their *bona fide* religious beliefs.[32] And as to abortion, the Christian doctrine that human life is sacred from the moment of conception has not received judicial support.[33]

VII. Conclusion

There is very little difference between understandings of freedom of religion from a secular standpoint, as opposed to a specifically Christian one, save that religious freedom particularly, and human rights more broadly, are generally understood by Christians as a gift of God. Christians assume for themselves a duty to promote human rights in civil society. For some, the duty is imposed by Church teaching, for others by Church law or guidance (soft law), and for many, by both. Whilst Churches benefit from collective human rights under civil law, they also assert in their internal regulation, claims to religious freedom in the form of institutional autonomy, and provide for cooperation with the State and compliance with secular legal provisions. However, the pattern which emerges is that the churches reverse the image of human rights in civil law when it comes to the regulation of their own internal affairs. Civil law begins with human

31 *R v. Secretary of State for Education and Employment and others ex parte Williamson* [2005] UKHL 15.

32 *Bull v Hall* [2013] UKSC 73.

33 *In the matter of an application by the Northern Ireland Human Rights Commission for Judicial Review* [2018] UKSC 27.

rights and moves to limits on their exercise. Church law begins with duties on the faithful and moves to wider rights of conscience.

Freedom of religion is a necessary element of the Christian faith. The State should recognise, promote and protect the religious freedom of churches corporately and of the faithful individually. The free pursuit of religious truth is a universal value and the State should respect and facilitate this. Christians should be advocates of human rights law for all in civil society. Churches should cooperate together in the promotion of such rights in civil society as part of the ecumenical enterprise for greater visible Christian unity. On the basis that all the faithful in a church are equal in dignity by virtue of their baptism, a church should promote human rights law which, in its current day iteration in the Universal Declaration on Human Rights. Article 1 of the Declaration serves as a constant and enduring reminder:

> All human beings are born free and equal in dignity and rights. They are endowed with reason and conscience and should act towards one another in a spirit of brotherhood.

This aspirational statement must then translate into a lived reality. As His All-Holiness the Ecumenical Patriarch Bartholomew himself so eloquently put it:

> We believe that the protection of religious freedom by the modern state of law, which ensures the fundamental conditions of the varieties of religious expression and the social presence of religious communities, makes the dialogue of religions possible and imperative. This dialogue frees religions from introversion which usually feeds prejudices against the different, contributes to the discovery and promotion of religions' common humanistic assumptions and acts as a bulwark against fundamentalism.

Address V

The Environment

Climate Change: An Ecumenical Imperative
(University of Notre Dame, 28 October 2021)

It is a unique privilege to stand before this assembly of university staff and students, as well as visitors from the region and all over the United States, in order to receive the preeminent honorary award of Doctor of Laws of the University of Notre Dame for the initiatives of the Ecumenical Patriarchate in response to the foremost challenge of our time, climate change.

...

However, this convocation occurs in the context of yet another global challenge. Both climate change and the coronavirus pandemic are rightly labelled as crises. You may be aware that the etymological root of the notion 'crisis' is a Greek word (*κρίσις*) that signifies 'judgment'. The truth is that we are all judged by our response to or rejection of defining moments in our lives. Ironically, the strategies used to dismiss climate change and COVID-19 adhere to a similar pattern and are adopted by the same people.

Both climate and COVID-19 therefore present us with an unprecedented problem but at the same time an unparalleled opportunity. This is why, throughout the world, we witnessed how the pandemic revealed the *best* in human nature, as well as the *worst* in human indifference. We observed how first responders were willing to sacrifice their lives for the sake of caring for and healing others. Yet we also noticed how some institutions and individuals stubbornly insisted on sustaining profits over people, while persistently championing their own rights over the safety of others.

This is precisely where the role of the Church becomes paramount. Because a Christian should always remember the vertical dimension *alongside* – and never at the *expense* of – the horizontal dimension of the social gospel. It is of course always difficult to maintain a delicate

DOI: 10.4324/9781032636740-14

balance between these two dimensions, but that is the message of the Cross, which marks the tension and intersection between the earthly and the heavenly.

In this respect, it is an important but humbling lesson that the Church has learned during this time: namely, that religion must function and serve in *connection* with – and never in *isolation* from – science. Faith alone will not overcome the problems of our time; but the challenges of our time will certainly not be overcome without faith. Research and medicine are gifts from God; they supply answers to the question '*how*?' Faith and theology are also gifts from God; they provide responses to the question '*Why*?'

The ultimate struggle for Christians is how we can translate the doctrine of the Holy Trinity as communion and the teaching about the humankind created in the image of God into the daily and practical life of the world. In other words, how can the kingdom of heaven be reflected in the reality of earth? What does liturgy look like when it is extended to the service of the world? In the 7th century, St Maximus the Confessor spoke of a 'cosmic liturgy'. This broader worldview is what enables us to imagine a world that is different to the one we have created or become accustomed to. It is the conviction that something which has not yet happened *can actually happen* with the cooperation of everyone and the synergy of God. It is, as the Letter to the Hebrews, says: 'the substance of things hoped for and the evidence of things not seen' (Hebrews 11:1)

Like climate change, then, the global crisis of the novel coronavirus has presented us with ultimate questions about life and death, sickness and suffering, as well as healthcare and justice. And what we are facing cannot naively be dismissed as a temptation or a trial. It is not some kind of punishment from God or threat from government. And it is certainly not a result of 'sin' or a revelation of the 'end'.

…

Similarly, protecting the natural environment is neither a liberal nor a sentimental response. It involves constant pain and forgiveness, unrelenting preference and priority for what we truly value, for what really matters. It is the spiritual and moral response, whereby we become a healing and transformative presence among our neighbours and on our planet.

This brings us to another critical dimension of climate change and COVID-19. It is what we call *the ecumenical imperative* of our response. We faith leaders are called humbly and patiently to cooperate with leaders in the scientific and academic worlds, as well as the corporate and political domains. This interconnectedness reminds us that the earth unites us beyond any doctrinal, social, or cultural differences. The power of ecumenical dialogue lies in opening up beyond ourselves and our own interests, beyond our confessions or religions. It means learning to speak the language of care and compassion. And creation care brings us divided, insulated believers before a common task that we must face together.

As you know, last month we issued a statement with our brothers Pope Francis of Rome and Archbishop Justin of Canterbury. It was the first time that the three of us have ever jointly signed an urgent appeal on the urgency of ecological integrity and sustainability. In our statement, 'we called on everyone to listen to the cry of the earth and to the cry of people living with poverty, examining their behavior and pledging meaningful sacrifices for the sake of the earth which God has given us'.

Because we are all called to make connections between hurting people and hurting the earth. When some 25 years ago we defined abusing the natural environment as sin, we were pleading for people to revise their conception of what is right and what is wrong. As human beings, for instance, we surely understand that we cannot hurt our brothers and sisters, that there are consequences to our actions – moral, social, and legal consequences. Why, then, do we not grasp the fact that there should be repercussions – moral, social, and legal repercussions – when we harm God's creation?

This is why we applaud efforts to expand relevant statutes of international law to include 'ecocide' defined as the unlimited and unlawful destruction of ecosystems through oil drilling and spills, industrial fishing and livestock farming, plastic pollution and mountaintop removal, but also nuclear weapons and testing. In the same framework, we also welcome the discussion in the Latin Code of Canon Law to include a provision calling every believer not only to avoid damaging creation as our common home, but to enhance the natural environment. This certainly echoes the Orthodox worldview that considers both ecology and canon law as applied ecclesiology or spirituality in practice.

. . .

9 From Crisis to *Kairos*

The 'Green Patriarch' and Environmental Law

M. Christian Green

It has become trite to refer to climate change and its effects on our environment as an 'existential' challenge. The predominant dominionist attitude to the earth in some Christian thought, according to which the Lord provides and humanity can simply use it up, has given way in Christian traditions to notions of stewardship and 'creation care'. The Orthodox Christian tradition has been no exception, especially under the leadership of His All-Holiness Ecumenical Patriarch Bartholomew I, known as 'The Green Patriarch'.

The Ecumenical Patriarch's concern for the environment seems part of a larger emphasis on social ethics nurtured under his leadership. If the mysticism and spirituality of Orthodox Christian tradition has at times seemed a world apart from the kinds of moral theology and social ethics that have developed in other branches of the Christian tradition, Bartholomew's tenure has signalled the development of a distinctly worldly ethics, with concerns for the environment and climate change at the core. If the Orthodox Christian tradition has not always seemed as present as other branches of Christianity and other world religions in international discussions of human rights, here, too, Bartholomew's leadership has prompted greater ecumenical engagement, working with fellow Christian and religious leaders around the world to address the challenges posed by excesses of human agency and their effects on the climate and environment. For those of us working in law and religion, it seems worthwhile to consider how his teachings from the Orthodox Christian tradition might inform our understandings of environmental law and policy.

In this set of reflections, I consider Ecumenical Patriarch Bartholomew's teachings on climate, environment, and social ethics and what these suggest for environmental law. First, I examine his pronouncements on climate change and the environment, which are not new, but go back to the 1990s. Second, I examine key points from Bartholomew's recent compendium of Orthodox social ethics, *For the Life of the World: Toward a Social Ethos of the Orthodox Church*, and how the references to 'life' and the 'world' seem not accidental, but reflective of an ecotheology at the

DOI: 10.4324/9781032636740-15

very heart of Bartholomew's larger social ethics. Finally, I apply these teachings to key themes and principles in environmental law. Overall, the trajectory that I trace in this examination of Ecumenical Patriarch Bartholomew and his lessons for environmental law follows how that law itself must shift from crisis to *kairos* in its orientation to meet the challenges currently before us.

I. Climate Change: An Ecumenical Imperative

On 18 October 2021, Ecumenical Patriarch Bartholomew delivered an address at the University of Notre Dame, titled 'Climate Change: An Ecumenical Imperative'.[1] Notably, the address was accompanied by the award of Honorary Doctor of Laws, an honour highly appropriate, given the Ecumenical Patriarch's foundational training in Orthodox canon law. In his address, Bartholomew began by locating the current climate challenge in the 'etymological root of "crisis" (κρίσις) … a Greek word signifying "judgment"', further observing that '[t]he truth is that we are all judged by our response to or rejection of defining moments in our lives'.[2] There is a connection here. Law, in its articulation of legal and moral norms, is deeply involved in judgments of all sorts.

The Ecumenical Patriarch also discussed the coincidence and coalescence of climate change and the COVID-19 pandemic in the same breath as presenting an 'unprecedented problem but at the same time an unparalleled opportunity'; as he described it:

> This is why, throughout the world, we witnessed how the pandemic revealed the *best* in human nature, as well as the *worst* in human indifference. We observed how first responders were willing to sacrifice their lives for the sake of caring for and healing others. Yet we also noticed how some institutions and individuals stubbornly insisted on sustaining profits over people, while persistently championing their own rights over the safety of others.[3]

The law, of course, plays a significant role in channelling our natures and inclinations toward appropriate ends and in determining how social systems of public health and capitalist economics sustain – or fail to sustain – us in times of crisis. For His All-Holiness, the COVID-19 pandemic and

1 Ecumenical Patriarch Bartholomew, 'Climate Change: An Ecumenical Imperative', in J. Chryssavgis, ed., *Global Initiatives of Ecumenical Patriarch Bartholomew* (Notre Dame: University of Notre Dame Press, 2023) xxxiv.

2 Ibid., xxxiv.

3 Ibid., xxxiv.

the climate change crisis present similar challenges to our collective willingness to sacrifice for the common good.

The Ecumenical Patriarch's underscoring of '*the ecumenical imperative*' of the climate crisis also recommends a similarly imperative mode in law, including both international law and canon law, in addressing the climate crisis response. On this point, Bartholomew observes:

> This is why we applaud efforts to expand relevant statutes of international law to include 'ecocide' defined as the unlimited and unlawful destruction of ecosystems through oil drilling and spills, industrial fishing and livestock farming, plastic pollution and mountaintop removal, but also nuclear weapons and testing. In the same framework, we also welcome the discussion in the Latin Code of Canon Law to include a provision calling every believer not only to avoid damaging creation as our common home, but to enhance the natural environment. This certainly echoes the Orthodox worldview that considers both ecology and canon law as applied ecclesiology or spirituality in practice.[4]

Thus, the law, at the national and international levels, but also in the Church, is a crucial means by which we are to express and enact policies based upon our obligation and our responsibilities to people and to the planet.

Toward the very end of his remarks, Bartholomew lifts from the recently published Orthodox Christian social ethics compendium *For the Life of the World* the observation that 'we are dependent creatures, creatures ever in communion, and hence we are also morally responsible not only for ourselves or for those whom we immediately influence or affect, but for the whole of the created order'.[5] That is, we are dependent on and interdependent with each other in our public life and relations, not independent bearers of private rights. We are creatures in communion, not mere subjects of markets that too often seem isolated from the right and the good. We are responsible not just for our own families and communities, but for the fate of the planet. To understand further the implications of this ecologically-infused Orthodox social ethic means for the law, it is worth looking at what that social ethic says about the role of law in preserving the environment.

4 Ibid., xxxvii–xxxvii.

5 *For the Life of the World: Toward a Social Ethos of the Orthodox Church*, 2020, par. 76.

II. For the Life of the World

For the Life of the World was published in 2020, following a multi-year drafting process by a commission appointed by the Ecumenical Patriarchate under the signature of Ecumenical Patriarch Bartholomew.[6] While the document is young, it seems likely to assume a landmark function analogous to the one assumed by Pope John Paul II's 1995 encyclical letter *Evangelium Vitae* (The Gospel of Life) in the Roman Catholic Church.[7] Much as that encyclical came to be deemed Pope John Paul II's most important encyclical for its distinction between a 'culture of life' and a 'culture of death', Bartholomew's commission and signature of *For the Life of the World* seems likely to have an equally definitive effect on Orthodox social ethics going forward.

In *For the Life of the World*, one learns that even as the beauty, splendour, and mysticism of Orthodox icons, hymns, and liturgy beckon the faithful to a higher plane of spiritual existence with God, so the Church is also very much an institution of this world. This includes participation in and adherence to the human laws that govern our world, even from a posture of spiritual alienage:

> The Church should, of course, seek to live at peace with all persons in whatever lands it inhabits, and to offer that peace to everyone; and in most cases, this requires obedience to the laws that exist in those lands. Even so, the Church remains in some sense always an alien presence within any human order, and recognises that God's judgment falls upon all human political power in some measure. Christians may and often must participate in the political life of the societies in which they live, but must do so always in service to the justice and mercy of God's Kingdom.[8]

This respect for law is to be manifest not only in adherence to the myriad laws and regulations necessary to administer particular societies, but to higher principles of human dignity, human freedom, and human rights. As the document further insists:

> Orthodox Christians should support the language of human rights, not because it is a language fully adequate to all that God intends for his creatures, but because it preserves a sense of the inviolable uniqueness of every person, and of the priority of human goods over

6 Online at: www.goarch.org/social-ethos

7 Pope John Paul II, *Evangelium Vitae* (The Gospel of Life) (Vatican City, 1995).

8 *For the Life of the World*, par. 9.

> national interests, while providing a legal and ethical grammar upon which all parties can, as a rule, arrive at certain basic agreements … Orthodox Christians must recognise that a language of common social accord, one that insists upon the inviolability of human dignity and freedom, is needed for the preservation and promotion of a just society; and the language of human rights has the power to accomplish this with admirable clarity.[9]

If there remains any doubt concerning Orthodox commitment to human rights principles, these are definitively dispelled by *For the Life of the World*. Human rights is the focus of an entire section of the document, and various paragraphs articulate the importance of human rights language, and conceptualise human rights as an important legal framework for understanding human dignity. Therein, Orthodox Christians are advised:

> It is not by chance that the language of human rights, as well as legal conventions and institutions devised to protect and advance those rights, notably arose in nations whose moral cultures had been formed by Christian beliefs. Today, we employ the concept of innate human rights as a kind of neutral grammar by which to negotiate civil and legal mechanisms for the preservation of human dignity, general liberty, social stability, equal rights for all … Orthodox Christians, then, may and should happily adopt the language of human rights when seeking to promote justice and peace among peoples and nations, and when seeking to defend the weak against the powerful, the oppressed against their oppressors, and the indigent against those who seek to exploit them. The language of human rights may not say all that can and should be said about the profound dignity and glory of creatures fashioned after the image and likeness of God; but it is a language that honors that reality in a way that permits international and interfaith cooperation in the work of civil rights and civil justice, and that therefore says much that should be said.[10]

The commitment to human rights is not, however, purely anthropocentric, but an ethic that binds human beings to one another and to the preservation of creation, that humans may also flourish under the wise stewardship of laws and policies aimed at preserving the planet, especially those creatures and persons who are most vulnerable upon it. As a key passage on science, technology, and the natural world puts it:

9 Ibid., par. 12.
10 Ibid., par. 61. See also, pars. 61–64: 'VII. Orthodoxy and Human Rights'.

> There is a close and indissoluble bond between our care of creation and our service to the body of Christ, just as there is between the economic conditions of the poor and the ecological conditions of the planet. Scientists tell us that those most egregiously harmed by the current ecological crisis will continue to be those who have the least. This means that the issue of climate change is also an issue of social welfare and social justice. The Church calls, therefore, upon the governments of the world to seek ways of advancing the environmental sciences, through education and state subventions for research, and to be willing to fund technologies that might serve to reverse the dire effects of carbon emissions, pollution, and all forms of environmental degradation.[11]

The judicious framing of laws and policies to this end is how humans participate as co-creators with God in the larger theology of the Church. Notably, *For the Life of the World* describes this framework, following an interesting recital of many examples of solicitude toward animals by Orthodox Christian saints. The language of human rights is therefore extended not only to other persons and creatures of the animal world, but also to water, air, and other natural resources which should be used judiciously and in stewardship in order to preserve the life of the planet.

III. Crisis, *Kairos*, and Lessons for Environmental Law

In his recent pronouncements on the environment, Ecumenical Patriarch Bartholomew has shifted from the language of crisis to the language of *kairos*. The term *kairos* is theologically significant, but it also has special significance for law. Specifically, Bartholomew has observed:

> As Orthodox Christians, we use the Greek word *kairos* to describe a critical moment in time, often a specific historical period with lasting repercussions and eternal significance. For humankind and the planet as a whole, now is our *kairos*: the decisive time in our relationship with all of God's creation, when we must respond in an opportune manner to protect life on earth from the worst consequences of human recklessness. May God grant us the wisdom to act promptly.[12]

11 Ibid., par. 76.

12 Ecumenical Patriarch Bartholomew, 'Environmental Justice and Peace', selected quotes. Online at: www.orthodoxcouncil.org/-the-green-patriarch-.html

In classical Greek, *kairos* was a word for time that was different from *chronos*, which referred to linear or sequential time. Instead, *kairos* was a critical moment, a breaking point, and even a point of inbreaking of the divine. Notably, in modern Greek, *kairos* is also the word for 'weather', which has become such a source of woe in our current *kairos* moment.

Kairos is not necessarily a term that sits well with the law, especially in common law countries, where law typically develops slowly through the gradual accretion of legislation and court decisions. While the law is often embraced by advocates of progressive social change and environmental awareness, the law itself is often an inherently conservative enterprise. Whether it is dealing with a crime, a tort, or an administrative rule, justice often comes after the fact as a retroactive response to a wrong rather than a great leap forward to the right and just. As the great American theologian, the Rev Dr Martin Luther King Jr observed: 'The arc of the moral universe is long, but it bends toward justice' – and so it is with law. Still, it is worth taking up Bartholomew's invitation to consider how a *kairos* theology of climate change might apply to and inform law.

IV. Regulation to Reduction: The Necessity of Sacrifice

Much of the apparatus of environmental law to date has worked within the framework of regulation and deregulation. Partakers in industries and activities that harm the environment often call for complete deregulation or offer pretexts of obeisance to regulatory frameworks, even as they seek to scale them back. In this framework, anti-environmental actors and advocates routinely cite constraints upon the liberty of landowners and corporations to do as they like. However the deregulatory framework, in relying more on voluntary agreements than government coercion, does not go far enough. It remains tethered to the laws of the market and prioritises economic interests of the powerful to the exclusion of attending to the needs of the vulnerable. Additionally, once environmental laws are on the books to protect clean air and water, govern appropriate uses of land and natural resources, mandate environmental quality assessments, and seek corrective action to clean up environmental damage, the question of enforcement remains.[13]

What the most ardent advocates of the environment now insist upon is the need not just to regulate – but to reduce. Specifically, we must not simply preserve and regulate the *status quo*, but we must reduce

13 For further observations on the problems of the regulatory framework, see M. Montini and M.C. Green, 'Christianity, Law, and the Ecological Crisis', in J. Witte, Jr and R. Domingo, eds., *The Oxford Handbook on Christianity and Law* (Oxford: Oxford University Press, forthcoming 2023).

carbon omissions, our use of fossil fuels and their by-products, and, above all, the steady creep upward in global temperature. But the law may be better at regulation than reduction. Anytime there is a demand for reduction, there may be claims of a taking – of property, processes, and profits available no more. This can lead to claims for compensation and making whole, when the point of a call for reduction is to make us whole with less.

Bartholomew has insisted, in his environmental teaching, on the 'need for an ascetic spirit that can be summed up in a single key word: sacrifice' as the 'missing dimension in our environmental ethos and ecological action'.[14] This is connected to the Orthodox Christian concept of *enkrateia*, or 'self-restraint'. Bartholomew tells us:

> [W]e are to practice a voluntary self-limitation in our consumption of food and natural resources. Each of us is called to make the crucial distinction between what we *want* and what we *need*. Only through such self-denial, through our willingness sometimes to forgo and to say, 'no' or 'enough' will we rediscover our true human place in the universe.

This kind of reduction, sacrifice, and giving up of harmful uses of our environment is also well-expressed in the Orthodox and wider Christian understanding of self-emptying or *kenosis*, for Bartholomew tells us: '*Kenosis* means *plerosis*; voluntary self-emptying brings self-fulfilment. All this we need to apply to our work for the environment. There can be no salvation of the world without the missing dimension of sacrifice'.[15]

V. Compliance to Conservation: Transformation of the Heart

To meet the current climate challenge, environmental law will itself need to be transformed in ways that focus more on the spirit than the letter of the law. The regulatory model focuses nearly exclusively on compliance, requiring the strong arm of the state in investigating and penalising anti-environment policies. Narrow regimes of compliance will need to give way to voluntary and mutually beneficial agreements between industries and populations. Proprietary rights of organisations to privacy of

14 Ecumenical Patriarch Bartholomew I, 'Sacrifice: The Missing Dimension', address at the closing ceremony of the Fourth International Environmental Symposium' (Venice, Italy, 10 June 2002). Online at: www.ewtn.com/catholicism/library/ecumenical-patriarchs-address-at-venice-3708

15 Ibid..

information will need to cede to the priority of knowledge in the public interest, so that non-governmental and civil society organisations can access the information needed to hold industries and governments to account through democratic participation in setting environmental policy. Above all, priority will need to be given to the needs of vulnerable populations, who are disproportionately affected by the ecological crisis. Ecologies of power will need to give way to ecologies of mutual solidarity, social justice, and the common good.[16] And the mentality will have to shift from compliance to conservation.

When we say that law has both a letter and a spirit, we mean that it is a product not only of the human mind and intellect, but of the human heart and will. Here, too, the words of Ecumenical Patriarch Bartholomew are instructive:

> We often refer to an environmental crisis; but the real crisis lies not in the environment but in the human heart. The fundamental problem is to be found not outside, but inside ourselves, not in the ecosystem, but in the way that we think.[17]

Even in a *kairos* moment, the transformation of the human heart in this way does not happen all at once. Instead, Bartholomew tells us, echoing King's remark about the long moral arc,

> We do not lack technical scientific information about the nature of the present ecological crisis. We know, not simply what needs to be done, but also how to do it. Yet, despite all this information, unfortunately little is actually done. It is a long journey from the head to the heart and an even longer journey from the heart to the hands.[18]

This is the nature of the journey that must take place from technical compliance to ecological conservation.

VI. Precaution to Prophetic

The precautionary principle is a principle of law that has been embraced in environmental law. At root, the principle is an approach to technological innovations that carry the risk of harm and require careful study and

16 For the compliance mentality in environmental law, see Montini and Green, 'Christianity, Law, and the Ecological Crisis', op. cit.

17 'Sacrifice: The Missing Dimension', op. cit.

18 Ibid.

review. As with the legal concepts of regulation and compliance above, it has the cast of being an inherently conservative principle. As the Rio Declaration of 1992 proclaimed:

> In order to protect the environment, the precautionary approach shall be widely applied by States according to their capabilities. Where there are threats of serious or irreversible damage, lack of full scientific certainty shall not be used as a reason for postponing cost-effective measures to prevent environmental degradation.[19]

Though it may strike some critics as overly conservative and an obstacle to progress, the precautionary principle can be seen as one of the more forward-looking principles of environment law. The principle also correlates with a point repeatedly emphasised in a joint environmental declaration of Ecumenical Patriarch Bartholomew and Pope John Paul II: the need to take account of limits and human finitude. Bartholomew warns repeatedly of the dangers of 'economic and technological progress which does not recognise and take into account its limits'.[20] Indeed, the Pope and the Patriarch further inveigh that 'we must regain humility and recognise the limits of our power and, most important, the limits of our knowledge and judgment'.[21] The humble heart knows its limits and takes precautions. What we need now is for precaution to become prophetic in the form of an ecotheology of climate change.

VII. Conclusion: The *Kairos* Challenge

Recent headlines have become more challenging. Report after scientific report augurs dire consequences for humanity if we do not halt rising temperatures within a time as yet uncertain, but which becomes ever more urgent. What will happen to the planet if the temperature rises 2°C, 1.5°C, or even a single degree? Is the year beyond which there is no return 2040, 2030, or sooner than that? The degrees and the time frame seem to get smaller and shorter.[22]

19 Rio Declaration on Environment and Development, UN Doc. A/CONF.151/26 (vol. I), 31 ILM 874 (1992), principle 15.

20 Pope John Paul II and Ecumenical Patriarch Bartholomew, 'A Code of Environmental Ethics', in Chryssavgis, ed., *Global Initiatives of Ecumenical Patriarch Bartholomew*, op. cit., 8.

21 Ibid., 9.

22 See Intergovernmental Panel on Climate Change (IPCC), 'AR6 Synthesis Report: Climate Change 2023', Synthesis Report for the Sixth Assessment Report during the Panel's 58th Session, Interlaken, Switzerland, 13–19 March 2023. Online at: www.ipcc.ch/report/sixth-assessment-report-cycle. S. Sengupta, 'A Clear Message from Science', *The New York*

We have seen that not just recently, but for three decades or more, His All-Holiness has been living up to his well-earned moniker: 'The Green Patriarch'. We have seen that the environment and the particular challenge of climate change are not only a focus of his ecumenical initiatives, but also at the foundation of his conception of the social ethics of the Orthodox Christian tradition. His environmental ethics are informed and imbued by the tenets of his theology – *enkrateia* or self-restraint, *kenosis* and self-emptying, and also *epikeia*, or equity and justice for the vulnerable. Bartholomew's social ethics is, indeed, one *For the Life of the World.*

We see in Ecumenical Patriarch Bartholomew's environmental ethic one that is not only shaped by a distinctively Orthodox Christian eco-theology, but one capable of informing key doctrines and principles of environmental law. Even in its often conservative posture, law remains a key means toward progress and articulation of global norms and expectations of enforcement. All this is necessary, Bartholomew tells us,

> Because – ΝΥΝ Ο ΚΑΙΡΟΣ – now is the *kairos* – the decisive moment in human history, when we can truly make a difference. Because now is the *kairos* – when the consciousness of the world is rising to the challenge. Because now is the *kairos* – for us to save the soul of our planet. Because now is the *kairos* – there is no other day than this day, this time, this moment.[23]

Times, 20 March 2023. See also S. Kaplan, 'World is on Brink of Catastrophic Warming: U.N. Climate Change Report Says', *The Washington Post*, 20 March 2023; D. Carrington, 'Global Heating Will Push Billions Outside "Human Climate Niche"', *The Guardian*, 22 May 2023.

23 Ecumenical Patriarch Bartholomew, 'Saving the Soul of the Planet', address at The Brookings Institution, Washington, DC, 4 November 2009. Online at: www.orth-transfiguration.org/wp-content/uploads/2016/09/HAH-2009-Brookings-Inst-talk-Nov-4-2009w.pdf

10 Climate Change, Christian Ethics, and Christian Theology

Ecumenical Imperatives

Frederick V. Simmons

Ecumenical Patriarch Bartholomew delivered 'Climate Change: An Ecumenical Imperative' upon receiving an Honorary Doctor of Laws from the University of Notre Dame for his leadership in confronting this 'foremost challenge of our time'.[1] Although brief and broad as befits its genre, the address is significant. Indeed, I will argue that it constitutes an important – albeit incipient – development of Orthodox Christian thought. In this Chapter I identify that development, illustrate its ethical import and proper limit, and explain what it indicates about Christian ethics and theology. Cumulatively, I contend that 'Climate Change: An Ecumenical Imperative' shows that Christian ethics and theology too involve ecumenical imperatives.

I. Recalibrating Orthodox Christian Conceptions of God's Supralapsarian Creation and Human Beings' Moral Obligations: The COVID-19 Pandemic

In his Notre Dame address, Bartholomew describes the imperative he interprets climate change to harbour as ecumenical in multiple senses. Most obvious, given the occasion, under Bartholomew the Ecumenical Patriarchate has been at the vanguard in discerning this imperative and forging appropriate responses to it. What is more, according to Bartholomew, this imperative applies beyond the Orthodox Church and religious communities generally to obligate scientific, academic, corporate, and political organisations and so proves especially extensive. Finally, Bartholomew maintains that this imperative requires these various domains to cooperate in responding to climate change and hence summons them to a kind of unity.[2]

1 Ecumenical Patriarch Bartholomew, 'Climate Change: An Ecumenical Imperative', in J. Chryssavgis, ed., *Global Initiatives of Ecumenical Patriarch Bartholomew: Peace, Reconciliation, and Care for Creation* (Notre Dame: University of Notre Dame Press, 2023) xxxiii–xxxvii.

2 Ibid., xxxvi.

DOI: 10.4324/9781032636740-16

Bartholomew acknowledges that such cooperation and unity have implications for Orthodox Christian practice. In particular, he insists that 'religion must function and serve in *connection* with – and never in *isolation* from – science' (italics original). Further, he reminds Orthodox Christians that '[r]esearch and medicine are gifts from God'.[3] Endorsing the natural sciences as complementing Christian practice and enriching Christian belief is not novel within Orthodox Christianity. On the contrary, this conviction is central to *For the Life of the World: Toward a Social Ethos of the Orthodox Church* (hereafter *FLOW*), a recent foundational statement of Orthodox social teaching.[4] Thus, it is fitting that Bartholomew cites this landmark document in concluding 'Climate Change'.

However, I have argued elsewhere that *FLOW* fails to appreciate the full ethical and theological significance of its encouragement of 'the faithful to be grateful for – and to accept – the findings of the sciences, even those that might occasionally oblige them to revise their understandings of the history and frame of cosmic reality'.[5] Specifically, although *FLOW* repudiates 'fideistic forms of Christianity that refuse to accept discoveries in such fields as geology, paleontology, evolutionary biology, genetics, and the environmental sciences', it denies that these fields' discoveries disclose the character of God's supralapsarian creation.[6] Instead, *FLOW* asserts that 'harmony, peace, communion, and abundance are the true "grammar" of creation', and it ascribes the strife, violence, death, and scarcity that these fields discover to creation's distortion by human sin.[7] Commensurate with this immense estimate of human sin's consequences for God's creation, *FLOW* claims that humans are 'morally responsible ... for the whole of the created order'.[8] After all, if human sin disfigured that order, *FLOW* concludes that humans have a 'vocation to transfigure the cosmos' by restoring the '"grammar" of creation' that they defaced.[9]

Christian scripture and the natural sciences arguably support a different conception of God's supralapsarian creation, the consequences of

3 Ibid., xxxiv, xxxiv–xxxv.

4 D.B. Hart and J. Chryssavgis, eds., *For the Life of the World: Toward a Social Ethos of the Orthodox Church* (Brookline, MA: Holy Cross Orthodox Press, 2020) Preface, pars. 55, 58, 71.

5 F. Simmons, 'Life in this World and *For the Life of the World*: Natural Science and the Social Ethos of the Orthodox Church', 78.4 *Theology Today* (January 2022) 385–395; *FLOW*, par. 71.

6 *FLOW*, par. 71.

7 *FLOW*, par. 42; see also *FLOW*, pars. 4, 44, 68, 77, 82.

8 *FLOW*, par. 76.

9 *FLOW*, pars. 73 and 42, respectively; see also *FLOW*, pars. 4, 5, 68, 69, 75, 82.

human sin, and the scope of human moral responsibility.[10] In particular, the canonical wisdom literature depicts God's supralapsarian creation as suffused by predation, death, and succession.[11] Likewise, the natural sciences discern these phenomena before human beings appear and describe them as integral to life's development, diversification, and sustainability. Correlatively, if these phenomena are aspects of God's supralapsarian creation, they are not due to human sin, and humans' moral obligation to repair their sinful distortion of that creation does not extend to redressing these phenomena.

'Climate Change' therefore constitutes a considerable advance in Orthodox thought insofar as it signals Bartholomew's embrace of this different conception of God's supralapsarian creation, the consequences of human sin, and the scope of human moral responsibility. That embrace first becomes evident in Bartholomew's discussion of the COVID-19 pandemic. According to Bartholomew, the novel coronavirus 'is not some kind of punishment from God or threat from government. And it is certainly not a result of "sin"'.[12] If not, that virus – and presumably other lethal pathogens – are evidently aspects of God's supralapsarian creation.

Bartholomew's interpretation of the crisis caused by the COVID-19 pandemic corroborates this inference. As Bartholomew observes, the word 'crisis' derives from a Greek term meaning judgment. Yet, while *FLOW*'s conception of God's supralapsarian creation portrays the novel coronavirus and other lethal pathogens as God's judgment on human sin, Bartholomew counters that the COVID-19 pandemic constitutes a crisis because people are judged by their response to pivotal events. Concerning that response, whereas *FLOW* commissions people to restore God's supralapsarian creation by transforming the cosmos, Bartholomew enjoins them to 'suppress' the pandemic and casts the human calling as 'reflecting' the kingdom of heaven 'in the reality of the earth'. In fact, Bartholomew presents Orthodoxy's celebration of a 'cosmic liturgy' as a way 'to imagine a world that is different from the one we have created or become accustomed to' rather than an expression of *FLOW*'s mandate to re-establish the world that God created.[13] In assessing the COVID-19 pandemic, then, Bartholomew assumes a conception of God's supral-

10 See further F. Simmons, 'Life in this World and *For the Life of the World*', op cit., 388–392 and F. Simmons, 'Augustinianism and the Book of Nature: Protestant Perils and Promise', in M. Harris, ed., *God and the Book of Nature: Experiments in Theology of Science* (Abingdon: Routledge, forthcoming 2024).

11 See, for example, W. Brown, *The Seven Pillars of Creation: The Bible, Science, and the Ecology of Wonder* (New York: Oxford University Press, 2010) 115–196.

12 'Climate Change', op. cit., xxxv. Of course, this assessment assumes the novel coronavirus did not emerge from a government administered laboratory.

13 'Climate Change', op. cit., xxxiv, xxxv, xxxvi.

apsarian creation that is less elevated – and arguably more aligned with scripture and natural science – than the conception that *FLOW* affirms. Correspondingly, Bartholomew depicts the consequences of human sin and the scope of human moral responsibility as less sweeping than *FLOW* envisions.

II. Qualifying Bartholomew's Recalibration of Orthodox Christian Conceptions of God's Supralapsarian Creation and Human Beings' Moral Obligations: Anthropogenic Climate Change

Bartholomew's conception of God's supralapsarian creation, the consequences of human sin, and the scope of human moral responsibility also informs his approach to climate change. In fact, he notes several salient similarities between the COVID-19 pandemic and climate change. For example, according to Bartholomew, both global challenges 'are rightly labelled as crises'; are dismissed by the same people using analogous strategies; pose 'ultimate questions about life and death, sickness and suffering, as well as healthcare and justice'; and, therefore, require an 'ecumenical response'.[14] I will discuss this ecumenical response in the latter two sections of this Chapter. First, I contend that Bartholomew's concentration on the similarities between the COVID-19 pandemic and climate change obscures important differences between them.

Although I commended Bartholomew's insistence that the novel coronavirus is not a result of sin as implying a conception of God's supralapsarian creation that departs from prior Orthodox ascriptions of nature's harmful qualities to human sin and so arguably aligns with Christian scripture and the natural sciences more closely, his failure to clarify that anthropogenic climate change is partially a result of sin suggests a conception of God's supralapsarian creation that dissociates nature's harmful qualities from human sin entirely. This suggestion is evident when several previously cited passages of 'Climate Change' are considered in context:

> Like climate change, then, the global crisis of the novel coronavirus has presented us with ultimate questions about life and death, sickness and suffering, as well as health care and justice. And what we are facing cannot naively be dismissed as a temptation or a trial. It is not some kind of punishment from God or threat from government. And it is certainly not a result of 'sin' or a revelation of the 'end'.

14 Ibid., xxxiv, xxxv, xxxvi.

> In fact, our response to COVID-19 is the very arena where all Christian believers – and, indeed, all people of good will – are called to be and struggle … Similarly, protecting the natural environment is neither a liberal nor a sentimental response.[15]

Given Bartholomew's refrain in 'Climate Change', that '[b]oth climate and Covid … present us with an unprecedented problem but at the same time an unparalleled opportunity', it is natural to interpret his reference to 'what we are facing' in this passage as including both climate change and the COVID-19 pandemic, and thus to infer that he emphatically denies that either are a result of sin.[16] After all, climate change *per se* is endemic to the earth system, the Holocene Epoch's remarkable climatic stability notwithstanding.[17] Moreover, even anthropogenic climate change is not simply due to sin but also arises from myriad legitimate human pursuits.[18] Nevertheless, while the novel coronavirus is distinguishable from the culpable human responses to it that exacerbated the COVID-19 pandemic, anthropogenic climate change cannot be disassociated from human responses to it since those responses contribute to that change.[19] And like human responses to the novel coronavirus, some human responses to climate change are culpable.[20] Thus, although anthropogenic climate change is not simply due to sin, it is not entirely free of sin either. Accordingly, while Bartholomew's ascription of some of nature's harmful qualities to God's supralapsarian creation is an important development of Orthodox thought, not all of nature's harmful qualities should be attributed to that creation.

This difference between the novel coronavirus and anthropogenic climate change likewise affects Bartholomew's interpretation of the judgment that the latter entails. Specifically, if climate change is 'rightly labelled' a crisis because people are judged by their responses to it as Bartholomew claims, then insofar as those responses contribute to this change, that crisis itself is also in part a judgment.[21] Further, inasmuch as

15 Ibid., xxxv.

16 Ibid., xxxiv.

17 See for example T. Lenton and A. Watson, *Revolutions that Made the Earth* (Oxford: Oxford University Press, 2011) esp. 351–362.

18 See for example W. Jenkins, *The Future of Ethics: Sustainability, Social Justice, and Religious Creativity* (Washington, DC: Georgetown University Press, 2013) esp. 16–45.

19 'Climate Change', op. cit., xxxiv. Again, this analysis assumes the novel coronavirus is not anthropogenic.

20 See for example N. Oreskes and E. Conway, *Merchants of Doubt: How a Handful of Scientists Obscured the Truth on Issues from Tobacco Smoke to Climate Change* (New York: Bloomsbury, 2010) esp. 169–215.

21 'Climate Change', op. cit., xxxiv.

the human responses that contribute to climate change have been sinful, the judgment that this crisis entails is negative. Consequently, this difference between the novel coronavirus and anthropogenic climate change affects Bartholomew's interpretation of the sorts of obligations that those who are culpably complicit in this change incur, too. In particular, once anthropogenic climate change is characterised as partially sinful, the vast normative implications that Bartholomew attributes to other kinds of culpable anthropogenic environmental degradation and destruction follow from culpable anthropogenic climate change as well.

Although he does not explicitly insist that anthropogenic climate change is partially due to sin, Bartholomew contends that this 'foremost challenge of our time' imposes a range of responsibilities, from 'protecting the environment', 'creation care', and 'cataly[zing] … ecological justice' to 'becom[ing] a healing and transformative presence', 'enhanc[ing] the natural environment', and even 'sav[ing] … our planet'. However, because he does not explicitly insist that anthropogenic climate change is partially due to sin, Bartholomew does not fully apply his admonition 'that there should be repercussions – moral, social, and legal repercussions – when we harm God's creation' to anthropogenic climate change. This restriction is apparent in his discussion of 'ecocide'. While Bartholomew 'applaud[s] efforts to expand relevant statutes of international law to include ecocide defined as the unlimited and unlawful destruction of ecosystems', he does not include anthropogenic climate change among the diverse examples he adduces to illustrate his remarkably broad interpretation of this crime. Since climate change is a paradigm of 'the unlimited … destruction of ecosystems', this omission evidently reflects Bartholomew's hesitancy to declare that change unlawful.[22]

In any case, just as Bartholomew refrains from forthrightly attributing anthropogenic climate change partially to sin, he stops short of attributing legal repercussions to that change. Accordingly, Bartholomew forebears from ascribing additional responsibilities to those most culpable for that change. Nevertheless, beyond the moral and social responsibilities that all incur amidst climate change, those most culpable for that change may be legally obliged to decrease their contribution to it. They may also be legally obliged to compensate those most affected by and least culpable for that change. Given his emphasis on the similarities between the novel coronavirus and anthropogenic climate change, Bartholomew neglects such legal possibilities. But whatever the legal regime, these differences between the novel coronavirus and anthropogenic climate change mean that while the consequences of human sin and scope of human moral

22 Ibid., xxxiii, xxxv, xxxvi, xxxvii.

responsibility are less sweeping than *FLOW* envisions, they are greater than Bartholomew indicates in 'Climate Change'.

III. Christian Ethics as an Ecumenical Imperative: Working with and Learning from Others

Despite eliding these differences between the novel coronavirus and anthropogenic climate change, Bartholomew rightly exhorts that both require an ecumenical response. After all, as inherently global realities, the COVID-19 pandemic and anthropogenic climate change can only be remedied with worldwide cooperation. This ecumenical response, in turn, has implications for the practice of Christian ethics. According to Bartholomew:

> We faith leaders are called humbly and patiently to cooperate with leaders in the scientific and academic worlds, as well as the corporate and political domains. This interconnectedness reminds us that the earth unites us beyond any doctrinal, social, or cultural differences. The power of ecumenical dialogue lies in opening up beyond ourselves and our own interests, beyond our confessions or religions. It means learning to speak the language of care and compassion. And creation care brings us divided, insulated believers before a common task that we must face together.[23]

For Christians, such self-transcending conversations and ethical unity across cultural and confessional differences properly begin within Christianity itself. Thus, in 'Climate Change' Bartholomew fittingly adverts to 'A Joint Message for the Protection of Creation', which manifests a welcome Christian ecumenism and eloquently exemplifies this cooperation.[24]

Yet, as Bartholomew instructs, the ecumenical imperative issued by the COVID-19 pandemic and climate change calls Christians to more than ethical unity amongst themselves. It mandates that they collaborate with others in forging concerted action across society's several spheres. Just as effective Christian ethical response to the COVID-19 pandemic requires contributions from medicine and public health, effective Christian ethical response to climate change requires contributions from the natural sciences, industry, and government. In addition, although it may be less

23 Ibid., xxxvi.

24 Ecumenical Patriarch Bartholomew, Pope Francis, Archbishop of Canterbury Justin, 'A Joint Message for the Protection of Creation' (1 September 2021). Online at: https://www.vatican.va/content/francesco/en/messages/pont-messages/2021/documents/20210901-messaggio-protezionedelcreato.html

obvious, the converse is equally true, for as Bartholomew perceptively observes, '[t]he challenges of our time will not be overcome without faith'.[25] Contemporary Christian ethics confronts inherently global realities. It must therefore learn from, coordinate, and complement a comparably encompassing set of human spheres and communities, and so issues an ecumenical imperative of its own.[26]

Furthermore, the multiple human spheres and communities that contemporary Christian ethics as ecumenical imperative would learn from, coordinate, and complement, must recognise their incompleteness if they are to cooperate in this way. Accordingly, as already implicitly noted, Bartholomew characterises the ecumenical imperatives elicited by the COVID-19 pandemic and climate change as entailing humility.[27] Beyond this, given the complexity and intractability of anthropogenic climate change, humility is needed to moderate the norms of and expectations for this imperative when addressed to that reality. However, given the fundamentally cooperative character of contemporary Christian ethics as an ecumenical imperative, this humility is also intrinsic to such ethics whatever realities it addresses. Indeed, because Christian ethics itself is essentially inclusive, it proves an ecumenical imperative not simply in response to the COVID-19 pandemic, climate change, or other inherently global realities but generally.[28]

IV. Christian Theology as an Ecumenical Imperative: A Conjunctive Mode of Reasoning about God and All Things in relation to God

Since it is a matter of reasoning about God and all things in relation to God, Christian theology itself is also essentially inclusive.[29] And since all

25 'Climate Change', op. cit., xxxiv.

26 For more on these multiple spheres and how contemporary Christian environmental ethics might coordinate them, see F. Simmons, 'Environmental Ethics and Christian Realism: Reckoning with and Hope Beyond an Era of Witting Ecological Ruin', in D. Gingles, J. Mauldin, and R. Miles, eds., *The Future of Christian Realism: International Political Decay and the Crisis of Democracy* (Lanham, MD: Lexington Press, 2023) 135–160.

27 'Climate Change', op. cit., xxxiv, xxxvi. For more on the role of humility in Christian cooperation with other disciplines, see R. Lovin, P. Danchin, A. Fuentes, F. Nüssel, and S. Pope, 'Theology as Interdisciplinary Inquiry: The Virtues of Humility and Hope', in R. Lovin and J. Mauldin, eds., *Theology as Interdisciplinary Inquiry: Learning with and from the Natural and Human Sciences* (Grand Rapids: Eerdmans, 2017) xiii–xxxiii.

28 See F. Simmons, 'Introduction: A Conjunctive Approach to Christian Love', in F. Simmons, ed., *Love and Christian Ethics: Tradition, Theory, and Society* (Washington, DC: Georgetown University Press, 2016) 1–3, 13.

29 Thomas Aquinas offers this influential definition of Christian theology in his *Summa Theologiae*, I.1.7.

things other than God are the subject of the non-theological disciplines, Christian theology too generally proves an ecumenical imperative insofar as the non-theological disciplines enrich and refine reasoning about other things' relationships to God.[30] Determining whether and how the non-theological disciplines enrich and refine such reasoning depends on learning from them. Consequently, like Christian ethics, Christian theology too requires humility.

Interpreting Christian theology as an ecumenical imperative is not new. For example, Augustine regarded empirical investigation as a key resource for Biblical interpretation and described empirical reality as 'the book of nature', a second medium of divine revelation that supplements the book of scripture.[31] Moreover, I have mentioned *FLOW*'s conviction that the sciences may offer theologically relevant insights. Yet, because the character of God's supralapsarian creation informs so many central Christian beliefs and the other disciplines mainly concern empirical subjects, these disciplines' potential to enrich and refine Christian theology is considerably greater when the character of God's supralapsarian creation is considered empirically accessible. Unlike many of his contemporaries and followers, Augustine considered the character of God's supralapsarian creation empirically accessible.[32] And as I argued in the first section of this Chapter, unlike *FLOW*, in 'Climate Change' Bartholomew evidently considers that character empirically accessible, too. Accordingly, Bartholomew's evident conception of the character of God's supralapsarian creation allows Orthodoxy to realise more of the potential for other disciplines to enrich and refine Christian theology and so fulfil more of that theology's ecumenical imperative.

In the first section of this Chapter, I described how Bartholomew's evident conception of God's supralapsarian creation alters *FLOW's* conception of that creation, the consequences of human sin, and the scope of human moral responsibility. In this final section, I outline how Bartholomew's evident conception of God's supralapsarian creation may enrich and refine Christian soteriology and eschatology. Given their commitments to God's power, wisdom, and goodness; monotheism; creation

30 See D. Ottati, 'A Collaborative Manner of Theological Reflection', in *Theology as Interdisciplinary Inquiry*, op. cit., 132–160.

31 Regarding empirical observation as enriching and refining Christian Biblical hermeneutics, see Augustine, *The Literal Meaning of Genesis*, I.19.39, I.21.41, II.9.20, V.8.23; Augustine, *Teaching Christianity*, II.16.24, II.29.45, II.39.58. Regarding empirical reality as the book of nature, see Augustine, *Reply to Faustus the Manichaean*, 32.20; Augustine, *Expositions on the Psalms 33–50*, 45.4.7; Augustine, *Sermons*, 68.6

32 See F. Simmons, 'Augustinianism and the Book of Nature', op. cit.

ex nihilo; and scripture's repeated attestation of God's acclamation of God's supralapsarian creation; Christians do not interpret God's salvation to deliver God's creatures from God's creation. Instead, they interpret God's salvation to deliver God's creatures from these creatures' distortion of God's creation. That is, Christian soteriology affirms God's salvation from sin and so implies God's restoration of God's creation to its supralapsarian character.

Correlatively, Bartholomew's evident departure from *FLOW*'s conception of God's supralapsarian creation and the consequences of human sin in 'Climate Change' entails a corresponding departure from *FLOW*'s soteriology. Specifically, while *FLOW* envisions God's salvation from sin to deliver God's creatures from strife, violence, death, and scarcity, and so restore them to the 'harmony, peace, communion, and abundance [that *FLOW* considers] the true "grammar" of creation', because Bartholomew's evident conception of God's supralapsarian creation attributes strife, violence, death, and scarcity to that creation rather than its distortion by human sin, a Christian soteriology informed by that conception does not envision God's salvation to deliver God's creatures from strife, violence, death, and scarcity.[33] Instead, it envisions God's salvation from sin to deliver God's creatures from injustice, torture, murder, and exploitation.

While such delivery would be a tremendous boon for God's creation and constitute a comprehensive transformation of society, it does not satisfy all Christian hopes. On the contrary, in failing to overcome death, privation, debilitation, and pain, this soteriology falls far short of what many Christians consider the crux of their gospel. Thus, if this soteriology were the full yield of interpreting Christian theology as an ecumenical imperative, for such Christians this interpretation would abandon that theology rather than enrich and refine it. However, Christian hope is not confined to soteriology but extends to eschatology as well. And beyond God's restoration of God's supralapsarian creation through salvation from sin, Christian eschatology includes God's consummation of God's creation. Accordingly, Christians who conclude that God's salvation from sin does not deliver from death, privation, disease, and pain need not infer that their hope for such delivery is misguided. Instead, they can cogently maintain this hope by attributing its fulfilment to that consummation.

Attributing more of the content of Christian hope to eschatology has significant pastoral, ethical, and political implications, some of which I have considered elsewhere.[34] Here I note that it explains Christians'

33 *FLOW*, par. 42.

34 See: Simmons, 'Life in this World and *For the Life of the World*'; Simmons, 'Environmental Ethics and Christian Realism'; and F. Simmons, 'How Theological Is Political Theology?

otherwise puzzling description of their eschatological hope as referring to God's consummation of God's creation. Given *FLOW*'s conception of God's supralapsarian creation, freedom from death, privation, debilitation, and pain does not consummate that creation but restores and preserves it. Given Bartholomew's evident conception of God's supralapsarian creation in 'Climate Change', however, such freedom consummates that creation by making all things new. In the first section of this Chapter, I claimed that Christian scripture and the natural sciences favour Bartholomew's evident conception of God's supralapsarian creation. It is now apparent that by characterising freedom from death, privation, debilitation, and pain as consummating God's creation, Christian theology does too. Eschatology, then, does not simply show how interpreting Christian theology as an ecumenical imperative enriches and refines that theology. It supports the conception of God's supralapsarian creation that both warrants interpreting Christian theology as an ecumenical imperative and allows this interpretation to enrich and refine that theology. Thus, insofar as 'Climate Change' affirms this conception of God's supralapsarian creation, it advances Orthodox Christian thought in both these ways as well.

The Case of Twentieth Century American Protestantism', 19.8 *Political Theology* (September 2018) 681–688, respectively.

Conclusion

Christopher Hill

This conclusion briefly recapitulates some of the themes which have arisen in this dialogue, between His All-Holiness the Ecumenical Patriarch Bartholomew and the contributors to this volume, on his legal thought and in his honour: canon law and ecumenism, Europe, human rights, religious freedom, and ecology. Inevitably, I have been selective and write with an eye to ecumenical ecclesiology as well as law. Issues for further exploration suggest themselves. I finally touch on the significance of the dialogue embraced by the contributors to this volume.

Aetios Nikiforos analyses Patriarch Bartholomew's significant contribution to Orthodox thought on canon law. He gives us not only a concise and focused account of the Patriarch's earlier studies but also their application by him from the Patriarchal Throne. In addition to calling for the codification of the Eastern canons (not least because some of them are no longer of practical utility or application), Patriarch Bartholomew argues for a way of understanding them which avoids both legalism and antinomianism. The Church is a 'divine-human' institution which requires law to safeguard ecclesial life. Yet evolution and change in law is required for the ultimate aim of 'serving the salvation and progress of the peoples'.[1]

Here the Orthodox practice of *οικονομια* (economy) is expounded, understood by Patriarch Bartholomew as essential to the whole Church, something lived rather than defined. Economy is the pastoral application of law which as context demands may mitigate the full rigour of the letter of the law. Economy ought not to be confused with the Western canonical principle of dispensation.[2] It demands unique application to individuals as persons. It is a fundamental pastoral stewardship which may require new canons as appropriate to our age. This tradition is dynamic rather

1 Nikiforos quotes the Patriarch who references Canon 12 of the Council of Trullo of 692, an Eastern Synod which completed the disciplinary work of the 5th and 6th Ecumenical Councils, sometimes for this reason called the Quinisext Council.

2 For a summary of different Orthodox views of economy, see W. Adam, *Legal Flexibility and the Mission of the Church: Dispensation and Economy in Ecclesiastical Law* (Ashgate, 2011) 23–33.

DOI: 10.4324/9781032636740-17

than static. On this basis, the Patriarch urges the comparative ecumenical study of canon law, not as defining difference but as clarifying basic agreement even with differing pastoral applications. I would cite the differing canonical provision for marriage and divorce as a case ripe for such comparative study, an area the Patriarch himself studied before he became a bishop. Nikiforos concludes with the Orthodox affirmation of ecumenical and inter-faith dialogue as expressed under Patriarch Bartholomew's presidency at the Holy and Great Council in Crete (2016). For such dialogue, the dynamic Orthodox principles of canon law provide a sure foundation.

Norman Doe references important statements which His All-Holiness has made on various occasions in relation to the principles of Christian law ecumenically. In arguing for the utility of principles of Church law, Doe outlines the story of the extraction of principles of canon law common to the Anglican Communion.[3] While the Ecumenical Patriarch has consistently encouraged the ecumenical study of canon law, this 'internal' Anglican exercise is a fascinating worked example of the distillation of such principles granted that the 46 (and five extra-provincial) Anglican Churches, from whose laws they are drawn, are juridically autonomous.

The work of the Ecumenical Christian Law Panel will also be a 'test case' for the positive feasibility of His All-Holiness' ecumenical vision. This vision is specifically to recognise the value of historic canonical principles for ecclesiology and for the ecumenical enterprise. For ecclesiology and the ecumenical movement, historic canon law in respect of the diocesan local church and its relation to other local churches is a major area for study and comparative examination. This is the foundation for the contemporaneous ecumenical emphasis on the *koinonia*, the communion of local churches. Here would be one area of study which would indeed, to quote Doe, be potentially 'a unifying force for global Christianity'. It would also be highly relevant to the tragedy of internal Orthodox divisions when the historic Orthodox ecclesiology of autonomous churches is over-ridden by the current aggressive nationalism of the Russian Federation.

The Ecumenical Patriarch has thought profoundly about religion in a changing Europe, and many of his ideas relate directly to the relevant laws involved. Frank Cranmer praises the significant contribution of the Patriarch to the 'great experiment of solidarity' which is Europe. Cranmer gives us an expert and accessible overview of the relation between the European institutions (not solely the European Union as such) and 'religion'. Cranmer stresses the Patriarch's consistent and regular insistence

3 *The Principles of Canon Law Common to the Churches of the Anglican Communion* (London: Anglican Consultative Council, 2nd edition, 2022).

on personal freedom, the free dignity and integrity of every human being. These are central values of the European project, itself founded by devout lay Christians in the aftermath of two World Wars. Miguel Blanco analyses the Patriarch's Europeanism and the various models of state-religious relations in the member states at national level. These models are of only relative value as each state has its own history of relations with religion. Blanco takes up Bartholomew's critique of the prevalence of a non-confessional model among European states. Rather than separation and neutrality, toleration and impartiality, as championed by the Patriarch, are required. Both Cranmer and Blanco note there is official dialogue between the European Union and 'religions' described as 'open, transparent and regular'. The extent to which a usually annual 'high level' meeting in Brussels really fulfils this ambition can, however, be questioned. On the basis of my experience in the past as President of the Conference of European Churches, this can become a 'tick box' exercise rather than a commitment to develop dialogue at all levels. For this to be fulfilled, more commitment is required in the institutions and states of Europe as well as within religious communities to work harder on the problem of the contemporary religious illiteracy of our societies, not least among religion's 'cultured despisers'.[4]

Cranmer and Blanco note that it is less easy now to be optimistic about the future of Europe, with the invasion of Ukraine. To this I would note the highly significant decision which the Patriarch made in 2019 to promulge the *Tomos* granting autocephaly to the Ukrainian Orthodox Church. That decision, itself a matter of Orthodox canon law, gives us a significant insight into the vision of the Patriarch. Europe is not monolithic and is comprised of many different cultural, political, social and ecclesial elements. There is to be no imperial dominance whether ecclesiastical or national. The Russian Orthodox Church has also apparently forgotten Canon 2 of the First Ecumenical Council which decrees that bishops should not intrude into other churches or provinces. In addition to the agony of Ukraine, it is establishing dioceses in places where there is already an Orthodox Church, such as in Africa where the Patriarchate of Alexandria has been established since Patristic times.

John Witte and Andrea Pin consider Patriarch Bartholomew's consideration of human rights. Witte appreciates the Patriarch's nuanced acceptance of human rights and sympathetically analyses the reasons Orthodoxy has been suspicious of Western (evangelical) missions in Orthodox territories. He considers the Orthodox and Byzantine tradition of the 'symphony' of Church and State which has never known 'two

4 For this phrase see Fredrick Schleiermacher, *On Religion: Speeches to its Cultural Despisers* (1799).

cities, two powers, two swords, two kingdoms, two realms'. He stresses that Western notions of separation or *laïcité* are over-simplistic. Both Witte and Andrea Pin, emphasise that human rights are not the invention of the Enlightenment or the French Revolution but have deep roots in the classical and canonical tradition. Liberty was before liberation. Pin focuses on the Patriarch's understanding of the dignity of human beings but also the importance of not understanding this as focused on the individual but rather the common good. He particularly emphasises Bartholomew's stress on a transcendent frame of reference for human rights. Both ask what the West can learn from Orthodoxy. Here, I would plea for further consideration, hinted at by the Patriarch, of the Orthodox anthropology of personhood as relational. A single 'person is no person'. This also corresponds with the widely accepted ecumenical ecclesiology of *koinonia*, communion; community in its profoundest spiritual sense rooted in the communion of the Holy Trinity. This has significant legal as well as ecumenical implications.

Isidoros Katsos gives an important analysis of Patriarch Bartholomew's own very significant thinking about religious freedom and human rights and its conciliar embodiment in the Holy and Great Council, Crete, in 2016. Katsos argues that the Patriarch introduced a new stance in Orthodoxy in terms of its epistemic approach to secular humanism which previously amounted to a rejection of Western human rights language as *inherently* individualistic. Katsos compares and contrasts the Patriarch's approach – and that of the Holy and Great Council – with the teaching of some Orthodox (specifically the Russian Orthodox Church) which strongly opposes an alleged Western ethical libertarianism. It is sad to note that the Russian Orthodox Church on this basis promotes itself as the true bastion of Christian values against not only a decadent West but also now among the Orthodox Churches. Katsos moves on to explore Orthodox attitudes to religious freedom, emphasising that Orthodox history has oscillated between being the Church of the powerful and the powerless and is critical of a too simplistic dismissal of the Byzantine Church–State synergy. Next, Mark Hill, like John Witte and Andrea Pin, argues powerfully that modern legal instruments enshrining religious freedom as pre-eminent among human rights owe more to the Judeo-Christian and other religious traditions than to the Enlightenment. Following Patriarch Bartholomew, he begins with the Edict of Milan before examining 20th-century evidence for this; Roman Catholic, Anglican, Lutheran, and the World Council of Churches. He also deals helpfully with the legal qualifications to the right of freedom of expression of religion.

Christian Green and Fredrick Simmons explore the Ecumenical Patriarch's longstanding environmental pioneering. In comparing his earlier teaching with more recent writings and the Orthodox compendium he sponsored, Simmons traces a development from the view that human sin is a distortion of the 'grammar of creation' to the conviction that not all evil is to be ascribed to sinful human agency, in particular the COVID-19 pandemic. Covid is not a punishment. This may imply that not all climate change is due to culpable human causes. Nonetheless, some changes may be so caused; and in any case, humankind has the duty to avoid 'ecocide' and wherever possible restore ecosystems that have been destroyed. Christian Green explores environmental law, noting that regulatory law centring on compliance will not be enough. Precaution must move to prophecy. Patriarch Bartholomew urges self-restraint, self-emptying and justice. On self-restraint, I would add the Orthodox spiritual (and canonical) tradition of fasting may have much to teach Western Christianity which in terms of actual practice has all but lost this tradition, including the Roman Catholic Church. Considerable theological and canonical preparation prior to the Holy and Great Council in 2016 were expended on this question.[5]

All the contributors to this book have affirmed the high value of His All-Holiness' personal contribution as an Orthodox theologian, canonist, bishop, and Patriarch to the precious Christian understanding of the free dignity of the human person in community and to freedom of religion in a multicultural Europe and wider world. Their analysis of his teaching is detailed and convincing, and on occasion constructively critical. In expressing their approval of his achievement they simultaneously support the Patriarch's contention that the comparative study of canon law is ecumenically advantageous. The book is itself an example of the method. The contributors rejoice in the Patriarch's canonical and ecumenical vision, now happily endorsed in the Cretan Holy and Great Council at which I had the privilege of being an ecumenical observer.

5 See N. Symeonides, ed., *Toward the Holy and Great Council* (Greek Orthodox Archdiocese of America, Department of Inter-Orthodox, Ecumenical & Interfaith Relations, New York, 2016) 57–73.

Index